THE MEDIEVAL LIBRARY UNDER
THE GENERAL EDITORSHIP OF
SIR ISRAEL GOLLANCZ, Litt.D., F.B.A.

Trobador Poets

Selections from
the Poems of
eight Trobadors
translated from
the Provençal
with Introduction
and Notes: by
Barbara Smythe

TROBADOR POETS
SELECTIONS FROM THE POEMS OF EIGHT TROBA- DORS: TRANSLATED FROM THE PROVENÇAL WITH INTRODUCTION & NOTES BY BARBARA SMYTHE

COOPER SQUARE PUBLISHERS, INC.
NEW YORK
1966

Published 1966 by Cooper Square Publishers, Inc.
59 Fourth Avenue, New York, N. Y. 10003
Library of Congress Catalog Card No. 66-23316

Printed in the United States of America
by Noble Offset Printers Inc., New York, N. Y. 10003

PREFATORY NOTE

THE following translations have been made from the critical texts of the songs of those Trobadors whose works have been separately edited. In cases where no complete critical text exists, the poems have been taken from Appel's *Provenzalische Chrestomathie*, from the collections of Raynouard and Mahn, and in a few cases from the MSS. in the Bibliothèque Nationale, Paris. The material for the Notes has been gathered partly from the Introductions, &c., to the special editions, and partly from general works on trobador literature. In addition to these I am indebted to Dr. Braunholtz's Cambridge University lectures on Provençal literature and to his tuition in the same subject.

Only a few inaccurately transcribed specimens of trobador melodies have been published ; my knowledge of the music is derived from the MSS. The neglect in which this very interesting and important branch of the trobadors' art has lain for so long has at last been repaired by Dr. J. B. Beck of Strassburg, who will shortly publish the complete musical remains of the trobadors. The introductory portion of Dr. Beck's work has already appeared.

The following is a list of works from which I have gathered materials for this book.

F. RAYNOUARD. *Choix des poésies originales des Trouba-dours.* 6 vols. (1816-1821.)

F. Raynouard. *Lexique Roman.*

C. A. F. Mahn. *Gedichte der Troubadours.* 4 vols. (1856-1873.)

C. A. F. Mahn. *Die Werke der Troubadours.* 4 vols. (1846.)

C. Appel. *Provenzalische Chrestomathie.* 2nd Edition. (1902.)

A. Stimming. *Der Troubadour Jeffroi Rudel, sein Leben und seine Werke.* (1873.)

G. Carducci. *Jaufre Rudel.* (1888.)

A. Stimming. *Bertran de Born, sein Leben und seine Werke.* (1879.)

A. Stimming. *Bertran von Born.* (1892.)

A. Thomas. *Poésies complètes de Bertran de Born.* (1888.)

L. Clédat. *Du rôle historique de Bertrand de Born.* (1877.)

U. A. Canello. *La vita e le opere del trovatore Arnaldo Daniello.* (1883.)

A. Kolsen. *Sämtliche Lieder des Troubadours Guiraut de Bornelh.* Parts I. and II. (1907, &c.)

A. Kolsen. *Guiraut von Bornelh.* (1894.)

C. Bartsch. *Peire Vidal's Lieder.* (1857.)

S. Schopf. *Beiträge zur Biographie und zur Chronologie der Lieder des Troubadours Peire Vidal.* (1887.)

F. Hueffer. *Der Trobador Guilhem de Cabestanh.* (1869.)

C. Bartsch. *Grundriss zur Geschichte der provenzalischen Literatur.* (1872.)

C. Chabaneau. *Les biographies des troubadours.* (1885.)

Dante Alighieri. *La Divina Commedia.*

Dante Alighieri. *De Vulgari Eloquentia.*

F. C. Diez. *Leben und Werke der Troubadours.* Revised by Bartsch. (1882.)

F. C. Diez. *Die Poesie der Troubadours.* (1883.)

A. Restori. *Letteratura provenzale.* (1891.)
J. H. Smith. *The Troubadours at home.* (1899.)
H. Suchier and A. Birch-Hirschfeld. *Geschichte der französischen Literatur.* (1900.)

For the initial letters of each chapter I have copied or adapted initials from two MS. collections of trobador poetry in the Bibliothèque Nationale, Paris, *fonds français* Nos. 854 (fourteenth century) and 12473 (thirteenth century). The design for the title-page is from MS. 22543 (about 1300); the figure from No. 854. For the frontispiece I have copied the melody and first stanza of a song by Bernart of Ventadorn (translated on p. 34) as they appear in MS. 22543.

BARBARA SMYTHE.

CONTENTS

Introduction

THE few Trobador[1] poems here translated form
a very small portion of the complete literary
remains of the mediæval lyric poets of Southern
France. Karl Bartsch, in his " Grundriss zur
Geschichte der provenzalischen Literatur,"
gives the names of four hundred and sixty
trobadors, most of whom have left some poems,
and the poems themselves number about two
thousand five hundred. These have been
preserved in MS. collections made in the
thirteenth and fourteenth centuries, a list of
which is given in Bartsch's invaluable work.
Many of these MSS. contain, besides the
poems, short biographies of the trobadors,
and two MSS.—Milan Ambrosiana R. 71
sup., and Paris Bibliothèque Nationale, fonds
français, 22543 — contain the melodies as well as the
words of some songs. Other Provençal melodies have
been preserved in MS. collections of old French songs.
A great deal of the poetry of the trobadors has been published,
the largest collections being those by Raynouard (" Choix
des poésies originales des Troubadours," six volumes) and

---

[1] The nominative form of the Provençal word is *trobaire*, from
hypothetical Latin, *tropator* (verb, *tropare*); accusative, *tropatorem*,
which gives *trobador*. The old French forms of the same word are
—nom. *trovere*, acc. *troveor*. In French the nominative form has
survived, as *trouvère*. The spelling *troubadour* is a French form
of the Provençal word, *trobador*.

Mahn ("Die Werke der Troubadours," four volumes, and "Gedichte der Troubadours," four volumes). Separate critical editions of the works of many trobadors have been published. The language spoken and written by the trobadors is now usually called "Provençal." Medieval chroniclers and poets generally used the name Provence to designate not only the province of that name, but the whole of France south of the Loire, and it was throughout this district that Provençal was spoken, though the dialect of Gascony differed so much from those of the other provinces as almost to count as a separate language. Provençal is not a mere dialect of French, but an independent language derived, like French, Italian, and most other languages of Southern Europe, from Latin. For political reasons it early ceased to be used as a literary language, and though it remained, and still remains, the spoken language of the people of Southern France, it came to be looked on merely as a patois. Of late years, Mistral and others have revived it for literary purposes. The modern Provençal written by them has of course developed from the language of the trobadors just as modern French has developed from the French spoken and written in the thirteenth century.

Among the mass of trobador poetry there is much that can be of interest only to philologists. Only a small number of the trobadors wrote poetry of any great literary merit. It would be difficult, however, to overestimate the literary importance of the trobadors as a whole, for it may be claimed for them that they were the founders of modern lyric poetry. Their songs were the first lyrical poems to be written in medieval Europe. The earliest specimens date from the end of the eleventh century, and during the next hundred and fifty years Southern France was the most important literary centre in Europe. The literature of Provence was imitated by the poets of Northern France, Germany, Italy, Catalonia, and Spain ; it was itself original. Yet the trobadors must have had some foundation on which to build up their art. This foundation must not be looked for in classical literature, to which Provençal poetry owes practically nothing. The songs of the trobadors were a native product. They represent a very self-conscious and artificial form of art which nevertheless had its origin, as far as we know, in the songs of the country people. It is supposed that the particular branch of popular poetry from which the trobadors derived their songs was the spring-song, sung, especially on the first of May, to accompany a country dance and to celebrate the return of the " sweet new season." Some of the spring-songs have come down to us, and though none of the MSS. in which they appear are earlier in date than the beginning of the thirteenth century, it is probable that the songs themselves are much older. They were very seldom written down, for they were not considered worth recording, and besides, they were intended merely to be sung, and were learnt by heart and handed down from generation to generation.

At the time when collections of French and Provençal artistic poems were first made, some of the old popular songs were included in the MSS., and so have been preserved for us. In the form of both verse and melody they have a certain resemblance to the artistic productions of the trobadors, though they are much simpler.

It must be remembered that the art of the trobadors consisted not only in the writing of verse but in the composing of music as well, and words and music, the two halves of the Provençal song, should, whenever possible, be studied together. Unfortunately, the number of tunes that has survived is very much smaller than that of the poems. There are only two hundred and fifty-nine of them, whereas there are nearly ten times as many songs the words only of which are now in existence. But this comparatively small number of melodies suffices to give us an idea of what the trobador music was like, and also to prove that many trobadors were not only distinguished poets but musicians of great talent as well.

It must not be supposed that the artistic poetry of the trobadors was simply a development and continuation of the old poetry; the popular songs continued to exist side by side with those of the trobadors. We cannot definitely say what was the immediate inspiration of the first trobador poetry. The political and social conditions of Southern France favoured the development of court poetry more than those of any other European State. The country was divided into a number of duchies and counties, the rulers of which were practically independent, though some acknowledged the overlordship of the French, and others that of the English king. Each of these feudal lords had his own court, at which he welcomed as many trobadors as cared to visit him. Before the period of trobador poetry had begun, it was customary for every great lord to have a number of minstrels, or " joglars " as they were called, at his court, and these joglars often became trobadors when it had become fashionable to make verses, addressing their poems to the wife of their patron.

The servile position of many trobadors may partly account for the attitude of respectful homage towards their ladies which is a characteristic feature of their poems. But the veneration of women which distinguishes this poetry is chiefly to be traced to the influence of the spirit of chivalry, which was a very important factor in the development of the literature as well as of the society of the age.

In the early days of chivalry its religious aspect was the most prominent, but as time went on the defence of women, which was one of the duties of a knight, came to carry with it a certain reverence for them, and serving a lady became an end in itself, existing side by side with the service of religion.

The principles of chivalrous love were carried out chiefly by the lesser knights and by poets, many of whom were of obscure origin, but whose talents had won them a certain position in society. The great barons of the country were too much occupied with political matters to have time to spare for the ceremonies and refinements of chivalrous love, though many of their number were trobadors; but among those who had no lands of their own, and who lived dependent on the bounty of some powerful lord, it was a recognised custom to pay court to the wife of their patron. The greatest boon that a knight demanded of his lady was a kind look or word, and for the sake of such a reward he would dedicate himself to her as a vassal would to his lord. Bernart of Ventadorn says in a charming verse: "And therefore, lady, have pity on your true lover, for I vow to you on my faith that I never loved aught so well; with hands joined and head bent I give and deliver myself to you, and if there should be a fitting moment, give me a kind glance, for I have very great desire for it."

Though this conception of chivalrous love first originated before the time of the trobadors, and was not in the beginning necessarily expressed in poetry, it soon came to be the theme of the new literature that was springing up. Feudalism and chivalry were the important factors in the creation of trobador poetry. The feudal system of life, the brilliant courts of the great barons where singers were welcomed and encouraged, gave the necessary material support to the art, and gave also, in the relation between vassal and lord, the model for the relation between trobador and lady. Chivalry, first the protection and then the adoration of women, supplied the inspiration.

So complete was the dependence of the trobadors on feudalism, that their poetry could not survive its fall. No one living at the close of the twelfth century, when the art and fame of the trobadors were at their greatest height, could have predicted that in a hundred years' time scarcely a trobador would be left. Yet this was what actually happened. The Albigensian wars ruined the independence of Southern France. The barons were either exterminated or deprived of their possessions, and so impoverished that they could not support the trobadors any longer, and the latter were obliged to wander into Italy or Spain to seek new patrons. It is true that they found generous support in these countries, but the national character of their poetry was lost; it had become a trade instead of a recreation, and was gradually more and more neglected. Thus ended the most brilliant and in some respects the most important epoch of medieval literature.

Though it is easy to understand that feudalism and chivalry between them could produce an artistic poetry derived from old popular songs, it must be conceded that they would scarcely have sufficed alone to bring that poetry to such a high level of excellence as it attained. This level could only have been reached by the aid of an inborn love of song among the natives of Southern France. This fondness for song has always been recognised as belonging to the Provençals. Philippe Mousket, the old French chronicler, accounts for it as follows. When the Emperor Charlemagne divided his lands among his adherents, he gave Provence to the singers and musicians; this was the cause of the love of melody and song which the Provençals have had ever since, and of their supremacy over all other people in music and poetry. This is a very fanciful way of accounting for the Provençal love of song, but there is no doubt that already in the time of Charlemagne the singers and musicians, the " joglars," were known and patronised in Southern France. The prosperous trobadors of the twelfth and thirteenth centuries had a certain contempt for the profession of joglar, but this profession was at all events of much greater antiquity than their own. These strolling entertainers were known in France from very early times. They went about from castle to castle and from town to town, earning what they could for their performances, which consisted not only in the playing of various instruments and the recital of long epic poems and shorter popular songs, but also in various juggling tricks. When trobador poetry became fashionable, the singing of the newest songs was added to the joglar's list of accomplishments. Trobador literature, far from causing a decline in the popularity of the joglars, proved an encouragement and a valuable addition to their profession. People were always ready to hear a new song by some well-known trobador ; and the poets themselves, though they often sang their own songs, were only too willing to teach them to the joglars, by whom they were quickly circulated throughout the country, and so brought fame and popularity to their authors. If a trobador could not sing well, he took a joglar into his service who went about with him and sang his songs. Some joglars wrote songs themselves, and thus rose to the rank of trobadors, while on the other hand those trobadors who had not the means to live as knights adopted the profession of joglar.

It may be well at this point to attempt some sort of definition of a trobador. As a matter of fact, the two classes of trobador and joglar were not always kept very distinct in their own time. The most general distinction was that a " trobador " was one who wrote original songs, while a " joglar " merely performed the works of others.

The word trobador is derived, according to Gaston Paris, from a term of musical art, *tropus*, signifying a melody, so that trobador means one who invents " tropi." Its derivation is more usually said to be from the verb *trobar*, to find (hypothetical Latin *tropare*), the meaning of *trobador* being literally a finder or discoverer.

Whereas all joglars, whether or not they were also trobadors, were, broadly speaking, a class by themselves, trobadors were of all classes. In the two hundred years—from the end of the eleventh till the end of the thirteenth century—during which trobador literature existed, we find kings and peasants, dukes and tradesmen, monks and joglars, all practising the art of song-making, and all brought to a sort of intellectual equality with each other by their art.

But though the poets were of all classes, the poetry was of one class only. The art of the trobadors was essentially of an artistic, not a popular, character. A great many rules had to be kept in the making of verse, and though these rules were not written down before the first half of the thirteenth century, they were regularly taught from an early period. There were no schools for the teaching of verse-making or music-making, but the trobadors learnt their art from each other. We cannot know who first made the rules. They were probably added to from time to time as the art developed, but, to judge from the careful form of words and music in early specimens of trobador song, some existed already in the time of the first trobadors.

It must not be forgotten that the songs were transformations of the old popular songs, and that some set verse-forms and melody-forms were borrowed directly from them.

There were many conventions and rules about the subject of the love-songs of the trobadors. The attitude of conventional homage which a trobador had to adopt towards his lady has already been touched upon. Patience and discretion were also necessary qualities. The identity of a trobador's lady was generally known, but nevertheless the most elaborate precautions were taken to keep it secret in theory at least. If the lady was addressed in the poem, a pseudonym had to be used instead of her own name, and a new song had always to be sent by a joglar or some other messenger, never brought by a trobador himself.

If the trobadors had little choice of subject in their poems, they could at any rate employ as great a variety of form as they pleased. It was a fixed rule that every new song must have a new melody and a new form, that it must differ either in the number and length of lines, in the arrangement of the rimes, or in some other particular from every song that had gone before it. All the stanzas of a poem had to be of exactly the same structure, as they were all sung to the same melody, but it was not necessary to keep the same rimes throughout. It was, however, customary to do so. It is not usual to find the rimes changing for every stanza as they do in most modern poetry, but not infrequently we find two stanzas or three written with the same rimes, and then a change. Sometimes the lines of a stanza rime not with one another but with those of the next stanza, and it is not unusual to find one line ending with a word which is repeated in the corresponding line of every other stanza. Some trobadors were not content with letting the last words only of their lines rime with one another, but made the lines rime in the middle as well. The subject of metrical structure is more fully treated in the notes to the translations.

In spite of all the rules which had to be kept in the composing of words and melodies, and of the fact that all their love-poetry was inspired by the same general idea, there is a wonderful variety in the songs of the best trobadors. There were, of course, a great many writers whose work never rose above mediocrity, and it would be difficult to distinguish the work of one such trobador from that of another, but we may say of others that they were really great poets. In the opinion of the trobadors' contemporaries, Guiraut de Bornelh was the greatest poet among them. Dante, on the other hand, and Petrarch after him, put Arnaut Daniel first. Most modern readers disagree with the Italian poets as to the relative merits of these two trobadors, and prefer Bernart of Ventadorn to either of them, but few will deny the title of poet to any of these three or to many others as well. Guilhem de Cabestanh, Peire Vidal, and many more, wrote poetry of great charm, and Bertran de Born, the turbulent sower of discord between Henry II. of England and his sons, was, in a different *genre*, one of the most remarkable poets of them all.

Very little is known of the lives of even the most celebrated trobadors. The contemporary " biographies," for the most part, give but the barest outline of the poet's life, and that is often incorrect, and the longer ones consist chiefly of anecdotes *à propos* of certain allusions in the poems.

Though we know next to nothing of their lives, we have at least enough of their poetry to be able to judge of their art. It is admittedly impossible to reproduce the exact effect of a poem in a translation; and trobador verse, especially the best specimens of it, should be read in the original to be appreciated. In the following translations, however, I have tried to give some idea of what these poems were like, both as to their exterior form and as to their spirit, though I fear very little of their poetry remains. I have reproduced the exact metrical structure of the originals in many translations, hoping thus to show the grace and ingenuity of some of the countless forms employed by the trobadors.   I can only hope that these translations, imperfect as they are, will help to show the reader that the old Provençal songs are interesting not only to the philologist, but to the lover of poetry as well.

oitou

THE art of the trobadors was not only fostered and encouraged by the nobles of Southern France, it was actually started by one of them. The earliest trobador whose poetry has come down to us was a powerful nobleman, Guilhem IX. Duke of Aquitaine, who was also Guilhem VII. Count of Poitou. Among the trobadors and their contemporaries he was always known simply as "The Count of Poitou." The familiarity with his art displayed by this poet, and certain allusions in his poems, show that he was not the only trobador of his time, but it may be safely assumed that he had no predecessors in the art, as no allusions to any earlier trobador are anywhere to be found.

Guilhem was born in the year 1071. The main facts of his life have been recorded by the chroniclers. In the year 1100 he went at the head of 300,000 men on a very ill-fated crusading expedition, of which he was almost the sole survivor. He is said by the chronicler Ordericus Vitalis to have made joking verses about his misfortunes in the East after his return, but unfortunately none of these have come down to us. Eighteen years later he started on an expedition against the Moors of Spain, and had a part in the great victory won over them by the King of Aragon

in 1120. In 1126 he was making war on the King of
France. In 1127 he died.

Several descendants of the first of the trobadors played
an important part in the literary history of the time. His
granddaughter, the celebrated Eleanor of Aquitaine, the
wife first of Louis VII. of France and afterwards of Henry II.
of England, was a liberal patroness of the trobadors, and
inspired some of the finest songs of the greatest of all Provençal poets, Bernart of Ventadorn. Her sons—Henry,
Richard Cœur-de-Lion, and Geoffrey, were also patrons of
the trobadors ; Richard even followed the example of his
great-grandfather, and wrote poems himself.

According to the chroniclers, Guilhem of Aquitaine was
a brave and accomplished, but also an irreverent and im-
moral man. Various anecdotes of him are recorded to
illustrate this character, and some of his songs further con-
firm it. Among the eleven which are extant some can
scarcely be looked on as examples of trobador verse ; their
bold coarseness suggests rather the inspiration of old popular
songs than that of the ideals of chivalry. He has, however,
left four love-songs of charming simplicity and sincerity.
These express a much less conventional and artificial emotion than we usually meet with in the songs of the trobadors ;
indeed the correct " feudal " form of love was not yet the
fashion, and even if it had been it is not likely that the great
Duke of Aquitaine would have troubled himself about it.
His thoughts were seriously occupied with political matters,
and poetry was to him only a diversion, not the chief busi-
ness of his life. Another of his poems is an " enigma," or
nonsense verse, a form of poetry which became popular
among the trobadors, who used it to express the dreamy
and confused state of mind to which love reduced them.
It cannot be said with certainty to whom any of his songs

were addressed, but it is probable that some at least were written to a certain Countess Amalberge, who was for some time his mistress.

The verse-forms employed by the Count of Poitou in his love-songs are simpler than some of those used by the later trobadors, but there is an ease and grace about them which show him to have been a practised poet. Of his talent as a musician we cannot judge, for except for a fragment of the melody to one of his songs which was adapted to different words in the Provençal mystery play of Saint Agnes, none of his music has come down to us.

I

Rejoicing greatly I begin
To love a joy I long to gain,
And since I turn to joy again
I ought to strive the best to win;
And better joy than mine within
The whole world I might seek in vain.

I, you must know, ought not to boast,
Or on my worth myself to plume
—But if a joy may ever bloom,
This should be perfect o'er the host
Of others, and bear fruit the most,
As sunshine brightens winter's gloom.

No joy could e'er imagined be
In man's desire, or in his mind,
Or in his thoughts, that I should find
Equal to this that's come to me.
No man could praise it well, though he
A whole year to the task assigned.

All happiness should bow before
My lady, all her power confess,
Because of her sweet graciousness
And of her beauty's goodly store.
He'd live a hundred years and more
Who could her love's great joy possess.

Her charm can cure the sick man's plight,
Her wrath can make the whole man die,
And make the wise man's wits to fly;
The fair man's beauty it can blight,
It makes the rudest boor polite
And makes the courteous rude and shy.

Since none can make a better choice,
Nor mouth describe, nor eyes behold,
I want her for myself to hold,
My heart to gladden with her voice,
And me to strengthen and rejoice,
That I may nevermore grow old.

If my belov'd her love will grant,
I am prepared to thank and take
And to dissemble for her sake,
And say and do whate'er she want;
Of her nobility I'll chant,
And all my songs for her I'll make.

To send no message do I dare,
Fearing her anger, nor do I
—So fear I to do wrong—draw nigh
To her, my passion to declare.
Yet she indeed for me should care,
Knowing my cure in her doth lie.

II

Now a ballad new I'll make me
Ere the winter overtake me ;
My beloved seeks to break me
Of my love—she doubts it's true.
But no word from her can shake me,
Never my bondage shall I rue.

To her power myself I've given,
May my chains be never riven,
'Tis no sin to be forgiven
That I love my lady true.
I should die if from her driven,
Hungering for her as I do.

Fairer than a flower her face is,
All else from my heart it chases,
And if very soon her grace is
Gained not, I shall die 'tis true,
But shall live if she embraces
Me 'neath the bough and kisses too.

Love, what gain will you be making
If, despairing, I'm forsaking
You—would you the veil be taking ?
Know, my love for you 's so true
That with grief my heart is aching
Till I receive amends from you.

How will you be better faring
If I turn a monk, despairing ?
—All the world's joy we'll be sharing,

Lady, if our love be true.
Now my comrade shall be bearing
My ballad unto her I woo.

Love makes me to freeze and tremble,
For I think it must be true
None whose grace did hers resemble
E'er from Sir Adam's lineage grew.

III

Enigma

A song of nothing I will write;
Not of myself or any wight,
And not of youth or love's delight,
    No, nor of aught.
On horseback fast asleep one night
    Of it I thought.

I've no idea when I was born,
I'm neither happy nor forlorn,
Nor friend nor stranger, I'll be sworn
    —'Tis destiny,
For thus on a high hill my Norn
    Decreed for me.

When I'm asleep I'm unaware,
Or when I'm waking, I declare;
My heart's near breaking with despair,
    With grief it faints
—And not a farthing do I care,
    By all the Saints.

I'm ill and like to die I fear,
But nothing know save what I hear;
I'll seek a leech, but far or near
   Find none I want.
If he can cure, I'll hold him dear
   —Not if he can't.

I've a sweetheart—I know not who,
I've never seen her it is true,
She's pleased me ne'er, done nought I rue,
   Nor do I care,
For messenger from her unto
   My house comes ne'er.

I've seen her ne'er, my love is mad,
She's never made me gay or sad,
When I don't see her I am glad,
   I care no straw,
For one who's fairer can be had,
   And worth much more.

To ask me where she dwells were vain,
If on a hill or in a plain,
How she wrongs me I can't explain,
   So none can know;
It grieves me sore here to remain,
   So I shall go.

My song of nothing's at an end;
To one I send it who shall send
It by another to my friend
   Down in Poitou,
That he to me may give or lend
   The riddle's clue.

NOTES

I. " *Rejoicing greatly I begin.*"

Metrical form.—That of the original is reproduced in the translation. The rimes in the original remain unchanged throughout
the poem, whereas I have changed them for every stanza.

II. " *Now a ballad new I'll make me.*"

Metrical form.—That of the original has been exactly preserved.
Note the recurrence of the refrain word *true* (in the original *am,
I love*) at the end of the fourth line of every stanza. The use of
such a refrain word was very common among the trobadors.

The short stanza at the end of the poem is called a *tornada.*
The structure of the tornada had to resemble exactly that of the
latter part of the preceding stanza—a rule that is not observed by
the Count of Poitou in this poem, for he changes his rimes. If a
poem had more than one tornada, the second might not be longer,
but might be shorter, than the first. The tornada was used by
most trobadors as an " Envoi." It was addressed either to the
lady who inspired the poem, or to a friend or patron, or to the
messenger who carried the song to the lady, or to the song itself.

III. " *A song of nothing I will write.*"

Metrical form.—That of the original is reproduced in the
translation except for the rimes of the short lines, which in the
Provençal are the same throughout the poem.

Stanza 2, l. 5.—This and other passages in trobador verse
(*cf.* especially the last stanza of Jaufre Rudel's song, " Whenas the
days are long in May ") allude to a popular belief in a species of

fairy godmother who arranged the destiny of mortals at their birth. I have doubts as to the suitability of introducing a Scandinavian Norn into a Provençal poem, but the exigencies of rime required her presence, and the *pairis* of the Provençals seem to have fulfilled a function similar to that of the lesser Norns of the Scandinavians.

returned from the Holy Land and wrote his remaining poems later. The second in date, according to Stimming, is "When the stream of the spring." Stimming thinks this was addressed to the same lady as "When the nightingale," but that it was written a good deal later than the latter, as it is much bolder in tone. Two more poems were written to this lady, but in the last of them the poet indicates that she has deceived him, and that he means to have nothing more to do with her. We cannot tell how soon after he began to dream of his unknown love in Tripoli. Perhaps the story of the Emperor's faithlessness inspired him to love the forsaken lady, as he had been thrown over himself. Of the "many songs" which, according to the biography, he made about her, two only remain to us. Translations of both are given below. The former of these two songs, "Whenas the days are long in May," is the most famous and the most beautiful poem by Rudel that we possess, but his poetry, tender and naïve as it is, is less poetical than the story of his love and death. It is not for his versemaking, but for his devotion to an ideal, that Rudel's name has been and will be known through the ages. No trobador's love-story is more romantic than his, and surely none had a more ideal ending.

> " O brother, the gods were good to you,
>   Sleep, and be glad while the world endures,
>   Be well content as the years wear through ;
>   Give thanks for life, and the loves and lures ;
>   Give thanks for life, O brother, and death,
>   For the sweet last sound of her feet, her breath,
>   For gifts she gave you, gracious and few,
>   Tears and kisses, that lady of yours." [1]

---

[1] Swinburne, *The Triumph of Time*, stanza 43.

I

WHEN the nightingale amid the leaves gives its love, and seeks it and takes it and sings its glad joyous song, and often looks at its mate, and the streams are clear and the meadows are smiling, then great joy comes to my heart because of the new delight that reigns.

I desire a certain friendship, for I know of no more precious joy ; I pray and wish that she may be kind to me and may make me a gift of her love ; for she is tall, slender, and fair, and her love and her understanding are good and without blemish.

I yearn for this love awake and, in my dreams, asleep, for I have a marvellous joy therein, wherefore I rejoice in it rejoiced and rejoicing ; but her beauty avails me nought, for no friend can teach me how I may ever have a good answer from her.

I am so desirous of this love that when I run towards it meseems that I go backwards and that it flies from me. And my horse runs there so slowly that scarcely shall I ever reach my goal, if Love does not hold her back for me.

I am desirous of a lady to whom I dare not tell my wish, but when I look on her face I am altogether bewildered. And shall I ever have courage to dare to tell her she may take me as her servant, since I dare not beg for mercy from her ?

Ah, how lovable are her words and how sweet and pleasing her deeds, for never was there born among us any woman so charming, slender and fresh and gentle-hearted, and I do not believe there is a fairer one, or one who so rejoiced those who looked on her.

Love, I depart from you rejoicing because I go seeking my good, and I am so far courageous that my heart will soon be rejoicing by the mercy of my good Protector, who wants me and calls to me, and deigns to help me, and has brought me back to good hope.

And whoever remains in comfort here and does not follow God to Bethlehem, I know not how he may ever be accounted noble or how he will ever come to salvation. For I know and believe of a truth that he whom Jesus teaches learns in a true school.

II

WHEN the stream of the spring grows clear as it is wont, and the wild rose appears, and the little nightingale on the branch turns and repeats and smoothes and beautifies its sweet singing, it is right that I should repeat mine.

Love of a distant country, my whole heart aches for you, and I cannot find a cure if I do not go at her bidding, led on by sweet love, into a garden or into a room with her whom I long for.

Since opportunity altogether fails me I do not marvel if I am enflamed by love, for never was there a fairer Christian woman, or Jewess, or Saracen, nor does God will it, and he who gains aught of her love is indeed fed with manna.

My heart ceases not to yearn for that lady whom I love best, and I think that desire deceives me if avarice takes her from me ; for the grief that is cured with joy is sharper than a thorn, so I never want any one to pity me for it.

Without a letter on parchment I send the song we sing, in simple Romance language, to Sir Ugon Brun, by Filhol. It pleases me that the Poitevin people and all Anjou and Guyenne and Brittany should rejoice in her.

III

WHENAS the days are long in May
I love the song of birds afar,
And when no more I hear their lay
Then I recall my love afar.
Sorrow so sore my heart doth blight,
Nor nightingale nor may-flower white
Can please me more than winter drear.

No more will love e'er make me gay
Unless I find my love afar ;
No fairer lady lives, I say,
In all the world, or near or far.
And all her virtues shine so bright,
For her I'd fain be captive hight
In heathen lands, and nothing fear.

Great joy 'twill be when I shall pray
From her a resting-place afar,
And if it please her, I shall stay
Near her, though coming from afar.
Ah, what sweet converse, what delight
We'll have when there our vows we plight,
When lovers far at last are near.

Happy and sad I'll make my way
When I shall see my love afar,
But yet I know not when the day
Will come, her country is so far ;
Full many a road leads there aright,
The distance doth not me affright
And unto God the way is clear.

My heart ne'er from the Lord will stray,
Who'll lead me to my love afar,
But for each joy I have alway
Two evils, for she is so far.
Would that, with staff and scrip bedight,
I as a pilgrim ever might
Before her beauteous eyes appear.

May God, Whose power the world doth sway,
Who did create this love afar,
Grant my desire, nor say me nay,
And let me see my love afar
Full soon, and this most joyous sight
Shall turn to day the darkest night
And give my grieving heart glad cheer.

He's right who says I'm yearning, yea
And pining for a love afar ;
No other longing I display
Save to enjoy my love afar.
But my desires are hopeless quite ;
Thus did my Fate decree in spite,
None should love me whom I held dear.

But my desires are hopeless quite ;
Curst be the Fate, whose cruel spite
Decreed that none should hold me dear.

IV

He cannot sing who sounds no air,
Nor without words a song compose;
Of rime, indeed, he little knows
Who has not learnt its rules with care.
Wherefore my song I thus prepare;
The more 'tis heard, its merit grows.

Let no man think it strange that I
Love one whom I shall ne'er behold,
No other love as dear I hold
Save hers on whom ne'er looked my eye,
Who's never told me truth or lie,
Nor know I if 'twill e'er be told.

She strikes a blow of joy that kills,
A wound of love that steals my heart,
Whence I shall pine beneath the smart
Unless full soon sweet pity fills
Her heart; no man with such sweet ills
E'er died, rejoicing, from love's dart.

I never fell asleep so fast
But that in spirit I was there,
Nor had, awake, such grief or care
But that my heart to her had past.
But when at morn I wake at last
Again of joy I'm unaware.

Never rejoiced I in her sight,
Nor will she e'er in mine; 'tis clear
That she will never hold me dear

Or vow or promise with me plight.
Ne'er laughed I so for sheer delight—
Yet what I'll gain does not appear.

Peironet, cross the Ili now
And I will cross to her, and she,
If she so please, shall shelter me,
And sweet discourse we'll have, I vow.
Full ill my Fate did me endow
If love for her my death will be.

The song is good if nothing wrong
I did, and all doth well accord.
Let him who learns it see no word
Is spoilt or altered in the song;
In Quercy 'twill be known ere long
By Bertran and Toulouse's lord.

NOTES

I. " *When the nightingale.*"

Metrical form.—The original is written in stanzas of seven lines, each line having eight syllables except the sixth, which is a feminine line and has only seven syllables. The rime-system is a b a b b cˇd. The last two lines find their rimes only in the corresponding lines of the following stanzas. The same rimes are used throughout the poem.

The music of this song is one of the most beautiful trobador melodies now in existence. Three other melodies by Rudel have come down to us, namely, those of the other songs here translated.

According to Stimming, this is the earliest song by Rudel that we possess, and the only one he wrote before starting on the Second Crusade. Stimming describes it as a crusading-song, but only the two last stanzas give it this character, the first six being entirely given up to the subject of the poet's love.

Stanza 7, l. 3.—" my good Protector." God, Who has inspired the poet with the desire to go on the Crusade and thus to do good to his soul. Or, according to Smith, who believes the Odierna theory, the "good Protector" is Odierna, and the poet in this song speaks of two loves, a lady of his own country and the far-off ideal princess.

II. " *When the stream of the spring.*"

Metrical form.—The rime-system of this poem is the most complicated to be found in Rudel's works. The stanzas contain seven lines of seven syllables each, the second and fourth lines having masculine and the others feminine rimes. The rime system of stanzas 1 and 2 is aˇb cˇd aˇcˇeˇ, that of stanzas 3, 4 and

5 is cˇd aˇb cˇaˇeˇ. The last stanza (the fifth) has the character of a tornada, both in its subject and in its form, which
reproduces exactly that of the preceding stanza.

Stanza 2, l. 1. " Love of a distant country." This looks like
an allusion to the " far-off love," but as other lines in the poem
suggest that the lady is known to Rudel, it is usually thought
to be addressed to his earlier love. In another poem to the
same lady he says, " Far are the castle and the tower where she
and her husband dwell," but in this poem it is clear that he
knows the lady of whom he writes, so we may suppose merely
that she lived in some part of France not very near to Blaye—
which is situated on the right bank of the Gironde, about twenty
miles north of Bordeaux.

Stanza 5, l. 2. Sir Ugon Brun is otherwise unknown. It was
customary among the trobadors not to write down their songs, but
to teach them to joglars, and send these to sing them to the persons
to whom they wished to make the songs known.

It would seem from the concluding lines that the lady was a
person of importance, since she was known even in Brittany.

III. " *Whenas the days are long in May.*"

Metrical form.—That of the original has been reproduced
exactly in the translation. The refrain word " afar " at the end
of the second and fourth lines of each stanza seems to insist on the
fundamental idea of the poem—the distance and the inaccessibility
of his love.

This song is at once the most famous and the most clear
expression of Rudel's longing for a far-off love. If his love-story
is indeed a myth, it was probably chiefly from this song that the
tale was invented.

The allusion to the land of the Saracens in stanza 2, and the
wish expressed in stanza 5, that he might go as a pilgrim to his
lady's country, explain themselves if we believe that the poem is
addressed to the Countess of Tripoli.

Stanza 7, l. 6. " Thus did my Fate." *Cf.* the note on

stanza 2 of the Count of Poitou's Enigma. See also stanza 6 of the following song.

IV. " *He cannot sing who sounds no air.*"

Metrical form.—In the original the rimes remain unchanged from stanza to stanza.

Clearly, this song is written about the Countess of Tripoli.

Stanza 6, l. 1. " Peironet." Probably his joglar. " the Ili." Most likely the Isle, a tributary of the Gironde, which any one travelling from Blaye to Marseilles—whence ship would be taken for the East—would in effect have to cross.

Stanza 7, l. 5. " Quercy." The province of Quercy belonged to the Counts of Toulouse.

l. 6. " Bertran." It is not known who Bertran is. A son of Count Anfos Jordan of Toulouse had this name. " Toulouse's lord." The reigning Count of Toulouse in 1147 was Anfos Jordan (1109-1148); in 1162, Raimon V. (1148-1194). This allusion to the Count of Toulouse understanding the song is considered, by those who believe Odierna to be the " far-off love," to prove that Rudel went on the Second Crusade with the Count. It can be quite well accounted for by the fact that the Counts of Toulouse and Tripoli were related, and probably kept up some intercourse with each other, so that the Count might know of Rudel's love.

ernart
of Ventadorn

LITTLE is known concerning this poet's life. His songs treat entirely of love, and contain no historical allusions, and it is only from the contemporary biography (never a very trustworthy authority), and from known facts concerning the persons with whom he came in contact, that we can construct the story of his life. Born probably some time between 1125 and 1128, he was the son of peasants in the service of the Viscount of Ventadorn in Limousin. The biography says "he was a man of poor birth, son of a servant who was an oven-tender, who heated the oven to cook the bread of the castle of Ventadorn"; and the trobador Peire d'Alvernhe, in a song satirizing his contemporaries, taunts him with having had a father who was a crossbowman, and a mother "who heated the oven and gathered fire-wood." What was really important for Bernart's after life was the fact that he was born in the domain of Ventadorn; as the Viscount Ebles II., the vassal and friend of the Count of Poitou, was himself a trobador, and soon discovered that the peasant boy had talent. He thereupon interested himself in Bernart, sent him to be educated at a monastery school, and himself taught him the art of song-making. And Bernart "became a fair man and a skilful, and he knew well how to compose and sing, and he was courteous and well-taught."

The Viscount Ebles III., son and successor of Ebles II.,
continued his father's patronage of the young poet, and
Bernart lived at his court and stood high in his favour. In
1148 Ebles married the beautiful Margarida of Torena
(Turenne), and Bernart and she fell in love with each other,
and he wrote all his songs for her. " And their love lasted
a long time before the Viscount or other men perceived it."
Many husbands tolerated and even encouraged the trobadors
who made love to their wives, but the Viscount was not one
of these. When we compare the passionate sincerity of
Bernart's songs with the artificial grace of many another
trobador's work, we need scarcely be surprised to hear that
the Viscount, when he discovered that his wife was the
subject of Bernart's songs, had her imprisoned and guarded,
and caused her to dismiss the trobador. It is almost impossible to believe that any of Bernart's songs were inspired by
the mere desire to offer conventional homage to his patron's
wife, and, whether Margarida cared for him or not, it is
fairly certain that he was in love with her. He seems to
have lingered near Ventadorn for some time, but soon he
journeyed northwards and took up his abode at the court
of Eleanor of Aquitaine, wife of Henry of Anjou, Duke of
Normandy. The "long time" during which the poet's
first love-affair lasted cannot have been more than two
years, for in 1150 Ebles III. repudiated Margarida, who
almost immediately afterwards married the Count of
Angoulême.

Bernart's affection did not long survive the parting from
his lady, for he was soon as deeply in love with the beautiful
Duchess of Normandy as he had before been with the
Viscountess of Ventadorn. Again, however, he was destined
to be parted soon from his lady, though this time it was a
political matter, not the husband's jealousy, which separated

them. In 1154 Henry of Anjou became King of England. It is probable that he took the poet with him when he went over to his new kingdom (see the Notes to the song, "When I see in the midst of the plain"), but Bernart soon returned to Eleanor in Normandy. The King himself soon followed him, and at the end of the year he took his Queen over to England to be crowned, "and Bernart remained on this side, sad and grieving." It is not known if he ever went to England again. He may have done so in 1158, but the biography tells us only that he went to the court of the "good Count," Raimon V. of Toulouse, and remained there till the Count's death. He then renounced the world and his art, and entered the Cistercian Abbey of Dalon, where he died.

Nothing is known of his life at the court of Toulouse. It is clear that he made a long stay there, as Raimon V. did not die till 1194, and he wrote some of his songs there, but we cannot even guess at the identity of the lady or ladies who inspired them. Bernart took great pains to conceal the námes of the ladies to whom his songs were addressed. Only a few songs can be assigned with certainty to the periods of his two known love-affairs. It is probable that those in which the lady is called "Tristan" were written to the Viscountess of Ventadorn, while the names "Conort" (Comfort), and "Aziman" (Magnet) refer to Eleanor of Aquitaine. The few songs which contain allusions to England and Normandy are also obviously addressed to Eleanor.

One fact seems fairly certain; though the poet had many different loves, his love was always real and not simulated. Through all his songs there runs a note of sincerity which is lacking in the work of many of the trobadors. The genuine emotion in his songs would alone make them worthy of study, but it is united with other qualities which make his poems the finest examples of trobador verse that we possess. Although one of the earlier Provençal poets, he possessed a complete mastery over form, and there is a wonderful richness and variety in the different metres he employs. Yet even in the most elaborately constructed of his songs, his language always remains simple and graceful. This simplicity of expression makes his poems easier to read in the original than those of almost any other trobador— it also makes them more difficult to translate. The following translations give but an inadequate idea of the work of Bernart of Ventadorn, whose songs, uniting perfection of form with grace of language and sincerity of emotion, entitle him to be looked upon not only as the greatest of the trobadors, but as one of the finest, if not the finest, of medieval lyric poets, and as worthy to be classed among the great writers of the world.

Forty-five of his poems have come down to us, and nineteen of his melodies. The latter show him to have been one of the best of trobador musicians. We can trace in some of them an effort to make the melodies suit the sense of the words.

I

WITH joy I now begin my song,
With joy I end and finish too,
And if the end be good and true
Then the beginning can't be wrong.
Since that for the good beginning
Joy and happiness I'm winning,
Therefore to thank the good end would be meet,
For all good things I hear praised when complete.

Joy masters and o'erpowers me,
And verily I marvel how
I can refrain from telling now
What joy is mine, and gaiety.
But 'tis seldom that a lover
Dares his passion to discover;
Fear of offending her makes me so meek,
My courage fails me and I dare not speak

I am well skilled in this one thing:
That willingly I always lie
To any man who asks me why
I'm happy, and rejoice and sing.
He acts foolishly and blindly
Who, when Love looks on him kindly,
Unto another dares his love to tell
—Unless he knows that he can serve him well.

I hate a meddling man above
All others, and it seems to me
There is no worse discourtesy
Than prying into others' love.
Envious, what are you enjoying,
Me thus troubling and annoying?
Let all men strive their duty to fulfil;
You gain no joy by treating me so ill.

Courage will oft a lady save
From spiteful and malicious men,
For if her heart do fail her then
She scarcely can be good or brave.
Her whom I shall love for ever
I implore that she will never

Be changed or moved by slanderous words, for I
Of jealousy can make the jealous die.

I never thought of treachery
When from her lips I tasted bliss,
But death she dealt me with a kiss,
And if one more she gives not me,
As by Peleus' weapon smitten
Shall I be, for it is written
That no man could be healed whom it had hit
Unless his wound was struck again by it.

Fair lady, I am conquered quite
By your great beauty and your fair
Red laughing lips and gracious air,
Sweet smile and eyes than stars more bright,
For, 'mong all I see around me
None so fair as you I've found me.
The gentlest lady in the world I woo,
My eyes are dazzled when I look on you.

Love with joy indeed has crowned me
Who to such a lady's bound me
That those who praise her cannot speak more true,
And those who blame, a worse deed cannot do.

II

WHEN the young grass and leaves appear
And flowers make the gardens gay
And nightingale doth sweet and clear
Upraise his voice and start his lay,
I've joy in flowers and joy in birds that soar,
Joy in myself, and in my lady more,

On every side by joy I am possest,
But she's a joy that conquers all the rest.

Oh I am dying of thought and care,
For oft I think upon her so,
Robbers might seize me unaware
And nothing of them should I know.
Ah Love, an easy prey in me you found,
With but few friends and to your service bound;
Will you not set my lady's heart afire
With love, ere I am dead of my desire?

I marvel that I can forbear
My passion to declare outright.
When I behold my lady fair
Her lovely eyes appear so bright
I scarce can bear to keep me from her side,
I'd hasten to her, feared I not her pride.
In face and figure none so fair I know
In loving so reluctant and so slow.

So well I love, so dear I hold,
So humbly serve, so sorely fear
My lady, that I am not bold
To speak or beg when she is near.
But well she knows my grief and misery,
And if she please, then she is kind to me,
And if she please, content with less am I,
So that no blame may come to her thereby.

If I were skilled in magic lore,
To children I'd transform my foes
Who then could trouble us no more
And nothing harmful could disclose.

Ah then I know that I should see my love,
Her shining eyes, her neck like plume of dove;
Then would my burning lips allay their drouth
And drink her kisses till they scarred her mouth.

Would I might find my lady when
She lies in slumber real or feigned,
For I would steal a sweet kiss then,
Which all my prayers have not gained.
Lady, by faith, love's gifts we little use,
And while time flies, its fairest hours we lose.
Let us converse in secret signals veiled;
Though courage help not, craft has never failed.

Now she who lets her lover stay
Long in suspense is much to blame,
For fruitless talk of love is aye
False and deceitful in its aim.
For one may love and feign to love elsewhere,
Tell clever lies when witness none is there;
Dear lady, if my true love you'd requite,
Falsehood should never give me doubt or fright.

Messenger, go, my friendship do not slight,
Though fear withholds me from my lady's sight.

III

WHEN I see the leaves falling from the trees, whomever it
   may grieve or trouble it ought to please me greatly.
   You need not think that I want to see flowers or leaves
   since she whom I most desire is harsh to me. I would
   fain depart from her, but I have not power to do it,

for I hope ever for her forgiveness even when I despair most utterly.

You may hear grievous news from me; when I gaze on the fair lady who was wont to welcome me, who now does not summon me or let me come to her, my heart is like to break with grief. May God, Who rules the world, let me rejoice in her, for if she opposes me thus, nothing will remain to me but death.

I trust no more in auguries or magic; good hope has ruined and killed me, for the fair lady whom I love so deeply cast me out when I asked her love, as if I had done her wrong. It grieves me so much that I cannot be comforted, but I do not show this, for I sing and pretend to rejoice.

I know not what more I can say, but it is great folly to love and long for the fairest lady in the world. He who first invented mirrors did worse than kill me, and it seems to me that I have no worse enemy; never when she looks at herself and sees her beauty shall I rejoice in her or in her love.

She may never give me all her love, nor would it be fitting, but if it pleased her to show me some kindness, I would swear to her on my faith that the favour she showed me should never be known through me; let it please her, for I am at her mercy; if it pleases her to kill me, I complain not at all.

Indeed it is right that I should lament if I lose through my pride the sweet companion and the joy which I was wont to have. My boldness gains me little since she whom I most desire has estranged herself from me.

Pride, may God destroy you, for now I weep through you! It is right that I should lose love, for I took it from myself through my own fault.

I know a very good way of lessening the loss and grief which I am enduring, for my thoughts are always with her; he who tries to move my heart and speaks of another does great annoyance and folly and rudeness; I have no better messenger in all the world, and I send it in pledge until I return from here.

Lady, I send you my heart, the best friend I have, as a hostage, until I return from here.

IV

WHENE'ER I see the lark take flight
And soar up towards the sun on high
Until at last for sheer delight
It sinks, forgetting how to fly,
Such envy fills me when I see
All those whom love thus glad can make,
I marvel that the heart of me
With love and longing does not break.

Alas, I thought I knew the art
Of love, but have it yet to learn,
For I to one have given my heart
Who ne'er will love me in return.
My heart she's stolen, and the whole
Wide world, and mine own self also,
And nought she's left me since she stole
Herself, but vain desire and woe.

My whole soul in her power lies,
My own I am not since the hour
She let me gaze into her eyes
As in a mirror full of power.
Mirror, I'm dying of despair
Since in your depths I first did look,
I lost myself, even as fair
Narcissus gazing in the brook.

Of women I despair; no more
In them will I put faith at all;
As I defended them of yore
So now do I renounce their thrall
And since I hold no other dear
Save her for whom I sorely grieve,
All I mistrust and all I fear,
For all are like her, I believe.

I blame my lady, for her deeds
Prove her a woman like the rest;
What she should like she scarcely heeds,
And what's forbidden she loves best.
None pities me in my distress,
And now a fool's reward have I,
Yet know not why 'tis so, unless
It be that I aspired too high.

Now of a truth is mercy lost
And never shall I know it more,
For she who ought to show me most
Shows none to me, though I implore.
Ill it beseems her that she should
Thus let her yearning captive die,

Who, save from her, can have no good,
And that her help she should deny.

Since with my lady naught avails,
Pity, nor justice, nor my right,
And since my love to please her fails,
I'll plead no more, but leave her sight.
Thus I renounce her utterly ;
She's slain me and she does not care,
And, since she wills it, I will be
An exile sad, I know not where.

Tristan, you shall hear nought of me,
I go away, I know not where,
Love I abandon utterly,
And joy and singing I forswear.

V

The nightingale rejoices among the flowers in the garden,
and such great trouble comes to me thereby that I
cannot help singing ; and I know not of what or of
whom, for I do not love myself or any one else, and I
make an effort because I know how to make a good
song when I am not a lover.

He who woos with pride and deceit gains more love than
he who is always supplicating and humiliates himself
too much, for love hardly wants any one who is frank
and true as I am, and has ruined me because I am not
false or deceitful.

For just as the branch bends whichever way the wind blows
it, so am I towards her who makes war on me, ever

ready to do her will. She plays and amuses herself well with me, for she fixes all her faults on me ; and indeed it is true that the thief thinks all men are his brothers.

She is always blaming and complaining of me and finding fault with me, and when she does anything foolish it is I who suffer for it, but what ruins and destroys me is that I am of low birth, for I will let her put my eyes out if she can reproach me for any other fault.

No man who saw her fair eyes or her face would think that she had a wicked heart or an evil will, but the water that flows quietly is worse than that which rushes. She who pretends to be gracious and is not, is deceitful.

I avoid and go away from every place where she is, and I pass before her with closed eyes that I may not see her. For he goes after love who goes away from it, and follows it who flies from it ; I have a very good mind to keep away until I return to my lady.

Never yet will I make complaint to her, although I am distressed, for it troubles me that I must yield thus and lose all my trouble. I keep and train myself for her service, and if we are not both friends, it does not seem or appear to me that my heart will be lightened by another love.

Tristan, though it does not seem so to you, I love you more than I am wont to.

VI

Since you ask me to sing, my lords, I will sing, but when I think to sing I weep whenever I try. You will scarcely find a singer who sings well when he is sorrowful ; but

I fare much better with love-sickness than ever I did, so wherefore am I dismayed ?

I know that God does me great good and great honour, for I love the fairest of ladies and she loves me, I know ; but now I am far from her and I do not know how she fares ; this kills me with grief, for I have no chance of going there often.

But it pleases me so well when I remember her, that, whoever cries or calls to me, I hear nothing ; the fair one draws my heart to her so sweetly that if any man says I am here, I think and believe he cannot see me.

Love, what shall I do ?   I am ever at war with thee, by my faith I shall die of desire which is in me if the fair lady does not let me come to her, that I may embrace her and kiss her, and caress her fair white body.

And therefore, lady, have pity on your true lover, for I swear to you by my faith that I never loved aught so well ; with hands folded and head bent I give and deliver myself to you, and if there should be a fitting moment, give me a kind glance, for I have very great desire for it.

I never grow tired of love through harm or trouble ; and when God is good to me I neither refuse nor scorn His goodness ; and if it happens otherwise I can well endure the sorrow, because a wise man must always draw back the better to spring forward.

My " Squire " and I have it in our hearts to go begging together, and that she should take with her him she loves without deceit, and I my Magnet.

VII

WHEN I see in the midst of the plain the leaves falling from the trees before the cold sets in and the summer departs, I want to make my song heard. For two years I have refrained from it, and now I must make amends.

Sorely it grieves me that I should ever adore her who hardens her heart against me; for if I ask aught from her it pleases her not to answer a single word. Indeed, my foolish desire is killing me, for it follows the fair semblance of love and cannot see that love fulfils it.

She understands deceit and evasion so well that I always think she is willing to love me; full sweetly she deceives me, for she ruins me with her kind glance. Lady, this is no gain to you, for I truly think the loss is yours whatever ill may happen to your servant.

May God Who protects all the world put it in her heart to welcome me, for food does not nourish me, nor any good thing profit me, so much do I fear the fair lady; wherefore I surrender myself to her, begging for mercy, so that she may give or sell me if she likes.

She will do ill if she does not send for me when she is undressing, that I may be at her command near to her at the foot of the bed, and may take off her dainty shoes humbly and on my knees if she will deign to hold out her foot to me.

The song is quite completed so that no word is lacking to it, beyond the land of Normandy across the wild deep sea, and if I am far from my lady, the fair one, whom God protect, draws me to her as with a magnet.

If the English King and Norman Duke wishes it, I shall
see her before the winter overtakes us.

For the King's sake I am English and Norman, and were it
not for my Magnet, I should stay till after Christmas.

VIII

THE nightingale's sweet plaintive air
When I have fall'n asleep at night
Wakes me, with joy bewildered quite,
Thinking of love and pondering.
And better I could not employ
Myself, for ever I've loved joy,
And I begin with joy to sing.

Of this joy I might well declare
—If of such joy one spoke at all—
That others' joys must seem but small,
And none with my great joy can vie.
And many a man will boast that love
Has favoured him all men above
Who has not half as much as I.

Oft I regard her beauty rare,
And see how lovely is her face,
How full her actions are of grace
—If to say more I had a mind
Then a whole year in very deed
Fitly to praise her I would need,
So courteous is she and so kind.

Lady, my arms for you I bear,
And e'er for you shall they be borne.

I am your vassal pledged and sworn
And evermore henceforth will be.
For first of all my joys are you,
And you shall be my last joy too,
As long as life remains to me.

Here I may seem to be, but e'er
My spirit with my love doth bide,
And moves not ever from her side
Although my body's far away.
My thought's a faithful messenger
And brings me joyous news of her,
And of her kindness day by day.

I know not when again or where
We'll meet ; I leave you sorrowing ;
For your sake I have left the King,
But pray to you this may not mean
A loss to me, for you shall find
Me humble, generous, and kind
At court with knights and dames, I ween.

Good Ugonet, pray bear in mind
The song that to you I've consigned,
And sing it to the Norman Queen.

IX

Such delight has come to me,
Reason it o'erpowers,
Frost and snowflakes seem to be
Red and yellow flowers,

For my joy grows mightily
With the wind and showers,
And my verse and melody
With fresh beauty dowers.
With love and with delight
My heart is flooded quite,
Winter seems like summer bright,
Snowdrifts leafy bowers.

Now, though all around me freezes,
I, in light attire,
Can defy the bitter breezes,
Warmed by true love's fire.
Overbearing pride displeases
Her whom I desire,
Humbleness in love more pleases
Me, since I aspire
To win love and delight
From her whose eyes' glad light
Is more precious in my sight
Than the wealth of Tyre.

Though her presence I must leave,
Far from her be hiding,
In her friendship I believe
Still with faith confiding.
If I see her, or receive
Of her any tiding,
On that day I shall achieve
Happiness abiding.
She is my heart's delight,
My soul to her takes flight,
I myself, unhappy wight,
Far in France am biding.

All my joy despair submerges,
Then, good hope returning
To my heart it bravely urges
Me to fear no spurning.
As a ship on ocean surge is
Ever tost and turning,
So my heart's great joy now merges
Into sorrow burning.
Now fled is my delight
—E'en Tristan, the true knight,
For Isolde and the night
Longed with less of yearning.

Would that I the form could take
Of a bird, then, flying
Through the night, my way I'd make
There where she is lying !
Lady, see, for pity's sake,
Your true love is dying,
And my heart is like to break
With my tears and sighing.
Oh, Queen of all delight,
I yield me to your might ;
Prithee now my love requite,
Make no more denying !

All my hopes and thoughts unbroken
Never from her part,
When I hear her praises spoken
Then by true love's dart
In my soul is joy woken,
Grief must needs depart,
And my happy face is token
Of my joyous heart.

I weep for sheer delight,
No grief my joy can blight
Nor my heart with sorrow smite,
Pain has lost its smart.

This song which I indite,
Go sing my love aright,
Let her know my piteous plight
Through my verse's art.

X

I CANNOT see the bright sun's glow,
So darkened to me is its light,
But this to me gives no affright,
For the fire of love is glowing
In my heart, which it has lightened,
And, though others may be frightened,
I am content, have what I want,
So my song in nought is wanting.

The fields that now are wrapt in snow
Seem to me filled with blossoms bright,
For now my joy is at its height
And I think, although 'tis snowing,
That the world by spring is brightened,
For my lady-love has heightened
My hopes and said her love she'll grant
—May she ne'er forget the granting!

From fear's advice no good I gain,
'Tis fear that makes the world so bad,
And wicked men, with envy mad,
Strive their purpose to be gaining

—How to make true love fare badly.
Cursèd men who act thus madly,
I would that God would all destroy
Who true love would be destroying !

And of such people I complain
Who make me sorrowful and sad,
For they are grieved when I am glad,
And whene'er they are complaining
And on others' joy look sadly,
I behold their grief right gladly
Since my delight can thus annoy
Those who oft are me annoying.

By night and day I weep and wake
And sigh, but soon I cease to grieve,
And count it joy ills to receive,
For good hope doth gently wake me
And it swiftly cures my grieving ;
Sure, 'tis joy I am receiving,
'Tis happiness e'en to desire
Such a love as I'm desiring.

Marvel not, lady, if I take
Such joy in you, but give me leave
To love you ; if you do, believe,
Happiness will overtake me,
Grief henceforth I shall be leaving
And all men will be believing
That to a high love I aspire
Since to yours I am aspiring.

XI

THE better to hide my sad thoughts and my trouble, I
sing and rejoice and show joy and happiness, and I
make an effort to sing and laugh, for I am dying and
I show no sign of it. And I am so overpowered by
Love, he has quite conquered me by force and by
battle.

God never made trouble or torment, except love-sorrow,
that I would not suffer quietly, but even that I endure,
though it grieves me, for Love makes me love wherever
he pleases, and I tell you this much, that if I am not
loved, the fault lies not with my slackness.

I am servant and friend and slave to my lady, and I ask
no other kindness from her but that she should secretly
turn her lovely eyes towards me, for her look does me
much good when I am sorrowful, and I will give her
praise and a thousand thanks for it, for I have no friend
in the world who is worth so much to me.

It is a happy day for me when I behold her, her mouth
and eyes and forehead and hands and arms, and her
whole person in which there is nothing that is not
beautifully fashioned. Beauty could make no one
fairer than she is, although I have great grief and
trouble from her.

I wish evil to my own will, so much do I desire her, and
I value myself all the more because I was so bold as to
dare to set my love in so high a place, wherefore I am
well-bred and prudent, and when I see her I am so
delighted that it seems to me my heart rises heaven-
wards.

Within my heart I am grieved and angry because I follow
my wishes so much, but no man ought to say such a
thing, for he does not know how fortunate he is. What
then shall I do about the fair secret glances? Give
them up? I would rather give up the whole world.

I have nothing to tell to slanderers, for great joy was never
kept hidden by them, and I tell you so much that to
excuse myself I have changed the dice by lying to them;
for every game is destined to be lost which is ruined by
their spying.

XII

I AM in thought and in trouble about a love which binds
me and looses me, for I cannot go so far this way or
that but that Love always keeps me in his control,
for now he has given me the heart and the will to beg,
if I may, for so great a favour that the King, if he
begged for it, would have shown great boldness.

Alas, unhappy wretch, what shall I do and what counsel
shall I take? For she does not know the grief that I
endure, nor do I dare to beg for mercy from her.
Poor fool, indeed you have little sense, for she would
noways love you in word or deed, but would see you
dead first.

And therefore, since I shall die thus, shall I truly tell her
the trouble that comes to me from it? Truly I will
forthwith tell it her—No, I will not, by my faith, even
if I knew I should gain the whole of Spain by it. I
would rather die a felon's death for its ever having
come to my thoughts.

Never through me shall she know how I suffer, nor shall another tell her aught of it. I want no friend in this affair, but may God ruin him who holds me back, for I want neither friend nor relative; for to me it is very great courtesy that love should kill me for my lady's sake, but it would not be honourable for her.

And therefore what wrong does she do to me, for she does not know what is happening? She ought indeed to guess by this time that I am dying of love for her.— And how?—By my foolish bearing and by my great cowardice, which ties my tongue when I come into her presence.

No joy is like to mine when my lady looks on me or sees me, for her fair, sweet glance goes to my heart which it sweetens and gladdens; and if it lasted long I would swear to her by the Saints that there is no other joy in the world, but I burn with grief at parting.

Since I will not send her a messenger and it is not fitting that I should speak to her, I know of no counsel to take, but I am greatly comforted by one thing; she knows and understands how to read, and it pleases me that I should write the words, and if it pleased her, she could read them for my salvation.

And if no other grief befall her, for God's and for mercy's sake may she not take away from me her kindness and her fair speech.

XIII

It is no marvel if I sing better than any other singer, for my heart draws me more towards love, and I am more obedient to its command. I have given up heart and body and wisdom and wits and strength and power to love, the bridle draws me so towards it that I care not a whit for any other thing.

He is indeed dead who does not feel some sweet taste of love in his heart; and what avails life without love, save to anger men? May Lord God never hate me so much as to let me live a month or a day after I have ceased to desire love and may be blamed as wearisome.

In good faith and without deceit I love the fairest and best of ladies; my heart sighs and my eyes weep, for I love her only too well, and lose much thereby. What else can I do? Love for her has seized me, and the prison in which it has put me can be opened by no key save mercy, and I find no mercy here.

This love wounds my heart so gently with its sweet savour: I die of grief a hundred times a day, and revive a hundred times with joy. Indeed, my grief is of fair seeming, for it is worth more than other good, and since my grief is so much good to me, good indeed will my joy be after my trouble.

Ah God! would that the true lovers were recognisable from among the false, and that slanderers and deceivers wore horns on their foreheads! I would give all the gold and silver in the world, did I possess it, for my lady to know how truly I love her.

When I see her, it is plain from my eyes, my face and my colour, that I tremble with fear as a leaf shakes in the wind. I have not as much sense as a child, so overwhelmed with love am I, and a lady should have great pity on a man who is thus conquered.

Good lady, I ask nothing of you save that you should take
me as your servant, for I will serve you as I would
a good master, whatever my reward may be. Behold
me at your command, faithful, humble, joyous, and
courteous; you are neither bear nor lion that you
should kill me if I give myself up to you.

I send the song to my " Courteous," there where she is,
and let it not displease her that I have tarried so long.

NOTES

I. " *With joy I now begin my song.*"

Metrical form.—That of the original is reproduced in the translation, but in the original the same rimes are used throughout.

According to Diez, this song is one of Bernart's earliest, being addressed to the Viscountess of Ventadorn, but we have no certain proof that this is the case. It is very characteristic in its expression of the writer's joy in the very thought of love and his outspoken hatred of the gossips and slanderers who were the bane of all the trobadors.

Stanza 6, l. 5. Peleus' weapon—the spear of Achilles.

II. " *When the young grass and leaves appear.*"

Metrical form.—That of the original is reproduced, except for the changing rimes.

Diez assigns this song and the following one to the period of the poet's love-affair with Margarida of Ventadorn. Both songs have very pretty melodies.

III. " *When I see the leaves falling.*"

Metrical form.—The original is written in stanzas of twelve lines ; feminine lines of five syllables and masculine lines of six syllables alternate with each other. The feminine lines of one stanza all rime together and the masculine lines do the same, but each stanza has fresh rimes.

IV. " *Whene'er I see the lark take flight.*"

Metrical form.—The original keeps the same rimes throughout. This song is one of the best known by Bernart, and the first stanza is looked upon as one of the brightest gems of Provençal poetry. The music also is especially beautiful.

The pseudonym "Tristan" is said by Bischoff to refer to the Viscountess of Ventadorn, but the general conception of the song suggests rather that, as Diez supposes, it was one of Bernart's latest. Many of his songs were written when he was in a despondent mood, but it is not usual to find him declaring that he will abandon love.

V. "The nightingale rejoices."

Metrical form.—The original is written in stanzas of eight lines, each line having seven syllables. The rime-system is a˘b a˘b cc d˘d˘. The same rimes are kept throughout.

This song has somewhat the character of an "Enigma," for in it the poet seems to defend his love in spite of, even because of, its unreasonableness. "Tristan" has obviously been unkind to him, but he is all the more ready to go on loving her.

Stanza 3, l. 5. "The thief thinks all men are his brothers." This is an example of the proverbial sayings that many trobadors introduced into their songs. In stanza 5 we find another, exactly similar to the modern French "Il n'y a pire eau que l'eau qui dort," and resembling the English "Still waters run deep."

VI. "Since you ask me to sing."

Metrical form.—The original is written in stanzas of nine hexasyllabic masculine lines. Rime system—a b a b a b a b b. The rimes remain unchanged for two stanzas; for the next two the *b* rime is used as the *a* rime, and a fresh rime is introduced for the *b* rime. A similar change takes place at the fifth stanza.

This song, which, from the allusion to "Magnet," we may suppose to have been addressed to Eleanor of Aquitaine, is one of the most charming that Bernart wrote. The fifth stanza gives charming expression to the idea that a trobador must swear fealty to his lady as a vassal to his lord. The effect of naïve sincerity is greatly increased in the original by the simple metre adopted, the nine short lines with their alternating rimes, However, as its simplicity of thought is the poem's most remarkable feature, and as it is easier to reproduce this in a prose than in a verse translation, I have not here attempted a metrical version.

Stanza 2, l. 3. "I am far from her." This allusion leads one to suppose that the poem was written when Bernart was in England, or possibly when the Queen herself had gone there.

VII. "*When I see in the midst of the plain.*"

Metrical form.—The stanzas have seven lines of seven syllables ; the fifth and sixth are masculine lines, the others feminine. Rime system, a˘b˘a˘c˘d d e˘. The second, fourth and seventh lines of each stanza rime only with the corresponding lines of the other stanzas.

This is one of the few poems the date and subject of which can be definitely decided. It furnishes the only proof we possess that the poet went to England ; the sixth stanza and the two tornadas show that it was written during his sojourn in this country with King Henry II. in 1154, when the King went over to claim his crown, leaving Queen Eleanor in Normandy.

Tornada 1. "The English King and Norman Duke." Henry II.

VIII. "*The nightingale's sweet plaintive air.*"

Metrical form.—In the original the same rimes are kept throughout. I have changed them from stanza to stanza, except for the first line of each stanza. These lines rime only with each other.

Probably the song was written after Bernart's return from England in 1154, as he says, "For your sake I have left the King." But apparently he was not at the Norman court, as he says he is far away from his love.

IX. "*Such delight has come to me.*"

Metrical form.—The metrical form of this song, perhaps the most beautiful that Bernart ever wrote, is as melodious as it is elaborate, and the complication of form hinders in no way the free and graceful expression of ideas. Although I have attempted a metrical translation in order to give some idea of the splendid swinging rhythm, I have not been able to reproduce exactly the rime system of the original. All the lines, except the ninth, tenth and eleventh, which have the refrain word *delight* (in the original *amor*, love), and its two rimes, should have feminine rimes, whereas the scarcity of feminine rimes in English has obliged me to alternate feminine and masculine lines, except in the fourth stanza. Then the last line of each stanza (and also the second, fourth, sixth and eighth) rimes with the first (also the third, fifth and seventh) of the following stanza, so that the effect of an unbroken but ever-changing chain of rimes is produced.

It is much to be regretted that the music of this song has not come down to us.

Stanza 2, l. 12. " The wealth of Tyre." What Bernart really says here is " Friesland " ; but as the city of Tyre is sometimes mentioned by the trobadors for its wealth, I have allowed myself to use the name here for the sake of the rime.

Stanza 3, l. 12. We may suppose, from the poet's saying that he was in France far away from his love, that the song was written after Queen Eleanor had gone to England to be crowned.

Stanza 4, ll. 10–12. Frequent reference is made by the trobadors to the loves of Tristan and Isolde, who were looked upon in the Middle Ages as the type of ideal lovers. It is interesting to note that though many trobadors compared their love and their faithfulness with Tristan's, they never presumed to compare their ladies with Isolde. There was too much equality in the love of the immortal lovers, too little servility on Tristan's part and too little imperiousness on Isolde's, to make it a fitting prototype for the loves of the trobadors and their ladies. In spite of this the story seems to have been the most popular, as it was one of the finest, of medieval romances, and it is therefore not surprising to meet with many allusions to it.

X. " *I cannot see the bright sun's glow.*"

Metrical form.—The versification of this song is noteworthy. It is written in what the Provençals called " derivative rimes," two

words derived from a common root, or different inflexions of the
same word, riming with two other words similarly connected.
The original poem is written on the same rimes throughout; in
the translation I have changed the rimes at every other stanza. It
is a proof of Bernart's genius that he was able to use this elaborate
device without any sacrifice of poetic effect.

It cannot be said to whom this and the three following songs
were addressed.

XI. " *The better to hide my sad thoughts.*"

Metrical form.—The original is written in stanzas of six decasyllabic lines, rime system aˇb aˇb b cˇ. The rimes remain
unchanged throughout.

XII. "*I am in thought and in trouble.*"

Metrical form.—The original is written in stanzas of eight lines;
the lines have eight syllables except the sixth and seventh, which
have only seven. Rime system, a b a b c dˇdˇc.

Stanza 7, l. 4. " She knows and understands how to read."
To be able to read was by no means a universal accomplishment
among ladies in the twelfth century, and it was not every trobador
who could write. Arnant Daniel says in one of his songs, "I
know well, without having the art of writing, what is a plain and
what a hill," &c.

XIII. "*It is no marvel if I sing.*"

Metrical form.—The rime system of this song is very complicated. The stanzas have eight octosyllabic masculine lines. The
rime scheme of the stanzas is: Stanza 1, a b b a c d d c; Stanza 2,
c b b c a d d a; Stanza 3, as 1, &c. This gives the intertwined
effect noticed in another of Bernart's songs. In spite of this
elaborate system, there is a naïveté and simplicity of thought and
expression in the poem, rendering it one of the most charming and
characteristic we possess.

ertran de Born

BERTRAN DE BORN, most famous of all trobadors, is a curiously different figure from any of his literary contemporaries. As they sang of love, he sang of war; as they tried to move the hearts of their ladies to pity, he strove to stir up the hearts of the nobles of France to strife and anger against each other. He wrote a few love-songs indeed, but it is by his war-songs that he has always been famous.[1] These have caused some few writers to hail him as a high-souled patriot, striving to free his native Aquitaine from the tyranny of her English rulers, but this is not the usual judgment passed on Bertran de Born. It was his fate to be stigmatised by Dante as an evil sower of discord, and he has gained the terrible immortality that a place in the *Inferno* gives to those who came under the ban of Dante's wrath. Dante's meeting with Bertran is thus described (*Inferno*, xxviii. ll. 118–142): "I saw indeed, and it seems as if I could see it still, a body without a head, walking as the others of the sad flock walked; and it held its severed head by the hair: it bore it in its hand like a lantern, and that looked upon us and said, 'O me!' Of itself it made a lamp for itself, and they were two in one and one in two; how that can be, He knows Who so com-

[1] The chronological order of Bertran's songs and their exact bearing on the events of his life have been decided differently by different commentators. I have followed the account of Bertran's life and the arrangement of his songs given by Stimming in his 1892 edition of the poet's works.

mands it. When it was right at the foot of the bridge it lifted up its arm with the whole head, to bring near us its words, which were: 'Now behold the grievous punishment, thou who, breathing, goest beholding the dead; see if any be great as this. And that thou mayst carry news of me, know that I am Bertran de Born, he who gave ill counsels to the Young King. I made father and son rebellious against each other; Achitophel did no more to Absalom and David with his accursed goadings. Because I parted persons thus joined, I carry my brain, alas, parted from its beginning which is in this trunk: thus is retaliation observed in me.'"

Had it not been for Dante's mention of him, Bertran's name might be less well known now than it is, but this passage in the *Inferno* has given him an unenviable notoriety as an unscrupulous sedition-monger, in which character he appears, for example, in Mr. Maurice Hewlett's romance of "The Life and Death of Richard Yea and Nay."

Probably the real Bertran was not as black as he is painted by Dante, who got his idea of the trobador from the Provençal explanations of his poems rather than from history. It is clear from his own songs that he loved war for its own sake, and it was this innate love of war rather than an evil desire to make mischief that led him to encourage the sons of Henry II. to make war on each other and on their own father.

More than one psychological study of Bertran has been written, but it is not likely that any more apt or truthful account of his life and character will ever be given than that of the Provençal biography. "Bertran de Born was a castellan of the bishopric of Périgueux, lord of a castle which was called Autafort. He was always at war with all his neighbours: with the Count of Périgord and with the

Viscount of Limoges, and with his brother Constantin, and with Sir Richard as long as he was Count of Poitou. He was a good knight and a good warrior, and a good wooer and a good trobador, and wise and fair of speech, and he knew well how to maintain good and evil, and he was master whenever he wished of King Henry of England and of his sons, but he always wished that they should be at war together, the father and the sons and the brothers one with the other. And he always wished that the King of France and the King of England should be at war together, and if they made peace or truce he always tried by means of his sirventes to show how each one was dishonoured by that peace ; and he had great good and great evil from the strife he stirred up between them."

The character thus naïvely described is clearly traceable in many of Bertran's own works, but though we cannot deny that he was contentious and bloodthirsty, we may claim for him that he was generous and a faithful friend, and that he hated anything in the nature of meanness and cowardice. He had a real affection for Henry II.'s eldest son, the "Young King," and if he abused him in his sirventes beginning, "I care not to delay longer in making a sirventes," it was because he was sincerely grieved to see his favourite weakly throwing away his chances instead of fighting for his rights. He does not seem to have had the same personal feeling for Richard, but, once he had accepted him as his master, he served him faithfully and spoke in no measured terms of the cowardly enemies who revolted against the King while he was in captivity. Though we cannot look upon Bertran as the champion of liberty, the precursor of Bertrand du Guesclin and Jeanne Darc, as some have made him out to be, we need not condemn him as altogether bad. He had some, at least, of the virtues as well as of the vices of his time. As for his political influence, whether good or bad, there has always been a tendency to overrate it. His name is not mentioned by the official chroniclers of the reigns of Henry II. and Richard I., so his part in the rebellions of the sons of Henry II. cannot have been considered a very important one. The history of his life may best be reconstructed from his own songs, the greater part of which deal with historical events of more or less importance, and from a few scattered references in the cartulary of the Abbey of Dalon and in the chronicle of Geoffroi de Vigeois (written in 1183). The Provençal " explanations " of the songs are delightful specimens of Provençal prose, but quite untrustworthy. Probably they were not written till about half a century after Bertran's death, and many of them are mere paraphrases of the poems. Allusions are often misunderstood, and curious blunders result.

The ruins of the castle of Born, in the department of Dordogne, probably mark the birthplace of the trobador. He was the eldest son of Bertran and Ermengarde de Born, and had two brothers, Itier and Constantin, the second of whom plays an important part in the story of his life. We cannot tell how and when he came into possession of the castle of Autafort. This castle originally belonged to the family of Lastours, and Constantin de Born married Agnes de Lastours, and later on Bertran's own daughter married a member of the same family. In an Act dating from some year between 1159 and 1169 Bertran and Constantin are described as possessors of Autafort.[1] Equally uncertain are the beginnings of Bertran's close relations with the sons of Henry II. of England.

[1] The existing castle of Hautefort, about twenty-one miles east of Périgueux, is built on the same spot as the fortress of Bertran de Born.

The English princes had lived with their mother in Bordeaux from 1163, and in 1169 Richard, the second son, had been made Governor of Aquitaine and Poitou, and was thus the overlord of Bertran de Born. It is therefore quite possible that Bertran took some part in the first revolt of the sons from their father in 1173, but there is no evidence to show that he did so. The eldest son, Henry, was crowned at Westminster in the year 1170, and was afterwards known as the " Young King." His discontent at having no power or possessions with his empty title led him first to think of revolting against his father. He was joined by his brothers Richard and Geoffrey, the latter of whom had become Duke of Brittany by his marriage, and King Louis VII. of France, together with many Aquitanian and French barons, united with them to try and overthrow Henry II. from his throne. As is well known the revolt was unsuccessful, and Henry II. compelled his rebellious sons and vassals to peace in the following year.

Though Bertran makes no mention of this revolt in any of his existing songs, it is thought that he may have taken part in it, partly because, in the oldest sirventes by him which we possess, " The Count has asked and incited me," Henry II.'s friend and ally, King Alfonso II. of Aragon, appears as the poet's enemy. This sirventes was written in 1181. The King of Aragon and the Count of Toulouse had a standing quarrel as to which of them had the better claim to the County of Provence. The King had an ally in Henry II. of England, who thought he had a claim to the County of Toulouse through his wife. A peace was patched up between the disputants in 1176, but war broke out again in the following year and was continued, without either party gaining any decided advantage, till 1181, when the King of Aragon brought a large army into the enemy's

country and appeared before the town of Toulouse. The
Count (Raimon V., whom we already know as the patron
of Bernart of Ventadorn) thereupon turned for help to
the Aquitanian barons, enemies of Alfonso and Henry,
and asked Bertran to write him a sirventes. It appears
from the Count's request that Bertran had already gained
some fame as a writer of stirring and effective war-
songs.

Bertran complied with Raimon's request for a song, but
did not himself take any part in the war, for his own affairs
were taking up his attention. He and his brother Constantin
were, not unnaturally, continually at strife over their joint
possession of the castle of Autafort, and about this time
Bertran succeeded in driving out his brother and in keeping
the castle for himself alone, whereupon Constantin went
to the Duke of Aquitaine to ask for redress.

Richard was himself at war with his own vassals. Since
1174, when his father had entrusted him with the overthrowing of those barons who refused to acknowledge the peace
of that year, he had reigned so cruelly as to induce his
vassals to revolt against him. A mutiny broke out early in
1182, the Viscount of Limoges, the Count of Périgord and
other nobles leaguing together against Richard, and Bertran
urging them on with his sirventes. Nevertheless, when
Constantin de Born came to him with his complaints against
his brother, Richard made peace with some of the rebels
and induced them in turn to unite with him and attack
the turbulent trobador, whom he looked upon, evidently,
as a dangerous enemy. Bertran, disgusted with his former
friends, who had turned against him, wrote a vigorous song,
"I have made a sirventes" (page 72). Richard besieged
Autafort, but abandoned the siege before long as his own
affairs were pressing. It seems from another sirventes,

" I delay not at all " (page 74), that Constantin went and laid his complaint before King Henry himself, but that Bertran cleverly succeeded in persuading the King of the justice of his own claim, and was granted the exclusive possession of Autafort.

Having brought his quarrel to such a satisfactory conclusion, Bertran now turned his thoughts in a very different direction. For a few months he gave up war and wrote nothing but love-poems. Maëut, his lady, was the wife either of the Count of Périgord or of the latter's younger brother Guilhem de Montagnac—probably of the former. Before Bertran had wooed her very long, he was rash enough to write a song in praise of the newly-married wife of the Viscount of Comborn, a lady celebrated for her beauty. Maëut, greatly annoyed, promptly dismissed her trobador, and Bertran thereupon addressed another song to the Viscountess, the beginning of which, " He who changes Good for Better increases his joy if he takes Better," was not calculated to appease the wrath of Maëut. Soon however he repented and addressed a poem to his first lady in which he justifies himself, and wishes himself all sorts of ill-luck if he is unfaithful as slanderers make him out to be. But Maëut was seriously offended and refused to forgive him. He next tried the effect of flattery, and explained in an ingenious song that he was going to ask every lady of his acquaintance to give him her most beautiful feature or grace, that he might make a feigned lady to console him for the loss of his Maëut, since there was no one to compare with her. When even this clever compliment failed to move her, Bertran went in despair to the lady Tibors, wife of the lord of Chalais, and offered himself to her as her trobador. Tibors promised to try and effect a reconciliation with Maëut, failing which, she said, she would accept the trobador herself. She was successful, and Bertran, forgiven at last, wrote a triumphant song. In the very same year, however, we find him singing the praises of another mistress. Henry the Lion, Duke of Saxony, who had married Mathilde, daughter of Henry II. of England, had been banished from his country for three years owing to his rebellion against the Emperor Frederic Barbarossa, and at the end of the summer of 1182 came with his family to Normandy to visit his father-in-law. Richard, having forgotten his quarrel with Bertran, asked him to come and cheer his sister in her exile, and Bertran spent the winter in the Norman court at Argentan and addressed two songs to Mathilde of Saxony. He admits that he was bored at the Norman court, and although the two songs to Mathilde are the best love-poems he wrote, it is clear that his homage was purely of a conventional order.

Bertran wrote no love-songs after 1182, but he often mentions his lady in his sirventes. The events of the following year gave him ample opportunity for indulging in his favourite occupation of stirring up feuds and urging on to battle.

The " Young King " had a quarrel with his brother Richard. He had asked his father for a duchy, and had demanded that his brothers should do homage to him as their future King. His father and his brother Geoffrey agreed to do what he asked, but Richard refused to do homage, considering himself, as Duke of Aquitaine, the immediate vassal of the King of France. The brothers were already quarrelling over the possession of the castle of Clairvaux, and the Aquitanian barons seized the opportunity of inviting the Young King to take the rulership of Aquitaine in place of Richard. Henry urged on by Bertran's gibes at his slackness, united with the barons, and war soon broke out.

At first the rebels gained the advantage, but before long King Henry II. came over from England with an army to make peace. The Young King consented to give up his demand, and the brothers swore peace. The Aquitanian barons were much disgusted at the failure of their plans, and Bertran wrote a sirventes, " I care not to delay longer " (p. 77), roundly abusing the Young King for tamely submitting to his father and leaving his friends in the lurch. The barons refused to acknowledge the peace, and soon young Henry, with his brother Geoffrey, went over to them again, and Bertran, at the Young King's request, wrote a stirring song for their encouragement. This second revolt, too, was doomed to failure, for young Henry fell ill of a fever, and died in Castle Martel on the 11th June 1183, having asked and received his father's forgiveness.

The rebels had nothing left to do but seek to defend themselves against the vengeance of Richard, whom they had sought to depose in favour of the Young King. Bertran, who wrote two of the most beautiful laments in Provençal literature in memory of his dead friend, shut himself up in Autafort, and Richard appeared before the castle on the 30th June, and took it a week later. Different accounts are given in the Provençal explanations of the manner in which Bertran received his pardon from Richard and his father ; and the real facts of the case are not known. The traditional story of how Bertran softened the heart of King Henry—a story which has helped to keep Bertran's name famous—is unfortunately a myth, for King Henry did not take part in the siege of Autafort ; but the version of it given, together with an account of the siege, in the explanation of one of Bertran's sirventes against the King of Aragon, is too good not to be quoted.

" King Henry of England kept Sir Bertran de Born be-

sieged in Autafort, and was fighting him with his battering-
rams, who wished him great evil, because he thought that
all the war which the Young King his son had made on him,
that Sir Bertran had made him do it, and therefore he had
come to Autafort to drive him out. And the King of Aragon
came with the army of King Henry before Autafort. And
when Bertran knew this, he was very glad that the King of
Aragon was in the army, because he was his special friend.
And the King of Aragon sent his messengers into the castle
to (ask) Sir Bertran to send him bread and wine and meat;
and he sent him plenty, and by the messenger by whom he
sent the presents he sent (a message), asking that he would
cause the battering-rams to be moved and drawn to another
part, because the wall where they were striking was quite
broken. And he (the King of Aragon), by reason of the
great riches of King Henry, told him all Sir Bertran's
message. And King Henry had more battering-rams put
in that part where he knew the wall was broken, and forthwith the wall was overthrown and the castle taken. Sir
Bertran, with all his people, was led to King Henry's tent,
and the King received him very ill, and said to him : ' Bertran, Bertran, you said that you never needed half your wits
at any time, but know that now indeed they are all needful
to you.' ' My Lord,' said Bertran, ' it is indeed true
that I said this, and indeed I spoke truth.' The King said :
' I think indeed that they have failed you now.' ' My
Lord,' said Sir Bertran, ' they have indeed failed me.'
' And how ? ' said the King. ' My Lord,' said Bertran,
' the day the noble Young King, your son, died, I lost my
wits and my sense and my understanding.' When the
King heard what Sir Bertran, weeping, said to him of his
son, great grief came to his heart and to his eyes for pity,
so that he could not prevent himself from fainting with

grief. And when he recovered of his swoon, he cried out
and said, weeping: ' Sir Bertran, Sir Bertran, indeed you
are right, and indeed it is fitting that you have lost your
wits for my son's sake, for he loved you more than any man
in the world; and I, for love of him, grant you your freedom
and your property and your castle, and give you my love
and my grace, and give you five hundred marks of silver for
the damage you have suffered.' Sir Bertran fell at his
feet, giving him thanks, and the King with all his army went
away. . . ."

Quite a different account is given in the explanation of
the song, " I am not at all discouraged " (p. 80). In this
song we have Bertran's own testimony to his having been
pardoned by Richard, who soon afterwards restored his
castle to him.

The episode marks a turning-point in Bertran's career.
Formerly he had been Richard's enemy, but now gratitude
made him his friend, and he served him faithfully from this
time forward. In the next year we find him singing in
Richard's behalf concerning a quarrel which had sprung
up between him and his youngest brother John, to whom
King Henry had suddenly demanded that Richard should
give up Aquitaine; and during the years next following,
his songs, treating of quarrels between the brothers and
between the Kings of England and France, were written on
Richard's side. Early in 1188 a new subject presented itself
to Bertran. In the preceding year news had reached
Western Europe of the defeats sustained by the Christians
in Palestine at the hands of Saladin, and of the conquest of
Jerusalem. Richard and Philip Augustus, the French King,
solemnly swore peace and friendship with each other, and
took the Cross; and Bertran praised their ardour and supported the proposed Crusade in a song, only a fragment of

which has come down to us. But Richard had no leisure
to start immediately on the Crusade. He had to punish
his vassal Geoffrey of Lusignan for the murder of a baron,
and immediately found himself confronted by a host of
rebels. No sooner had he quelled their revolt than he
heard that the Count of Toulouse had imprisoned some
Aquitanian merchants. To revenge himself upon the
Count he fell upon the latter's province of Quercy, took its
capital, Cahors, and the whole province, and then marched
into the province of Toulouse itself. The Count of
Toulouse turned to his overlord, the King of France, for
help. Bertran's delight in the prospect of a war is expressed
in two songs, " I cannot resist spreading a song " (p. 83),
and " If I were so much lord and master of myself " (p. 85),
both of which refer to these events. He abuses the French
King, whom he never liked, for his cowardice and slackness
in not opposing Richard. Philip Augustus began to make
war on Richard in the middle of June 1189. On the 6th
July Henry II. of England died, and Richard, now King,
turned his attention to securing his power throughout his
domains. Soon after his accession, Bertran wrote a song
reproaching both Richard and Philip with failing to keep
their vow of starting on a Crusade. This song, " Now I
know who has the greatest worth " (p. 86), is addressed to the
Marquis Conrad of Montferrat, who had gained some
victories in the Holy Land against Saladin. Richard had
always been anxious to go on the Crusade, and at the end of
the year he and Philip again swore mutual friendship, and
the expedition started in the following year.

Bertran took no part in the Crusade. As he explains,
he was too poor to " make war for long without wealth."
Moreover, though he encouraged the kings to take part in
the Holy War as a means of displaying their prowess, he was

himself more interested in the events of his own neighbourhood, which were always liable to influence his fortunes.
The song, " Willingly would I make a sirventes " (p. 88),
probably dates from a period soon after the Crusade had
started, for it contains complaints of the state of France,
whence the flower of the nobility had departed, leaving no
one to make war or to hold feasts.　France in these days
seemed dull to Bertran, but later on he had still more reason
to complain.　While Richard, who had been captured by
his enemy, Duke Leopold of Austria, on his way home from
the Crusade, was being kept in captivity by the Emperor,
the Aquitanian barons seized the chance of revolting against
his *locum tenens*.　Bertran was very indignant at this
cowardly proceeding, and expressed his feelings with his
usual vigour.　The news of the King's release was hailed by
him with delight, and when Richard was expected back in
France in May 1194, he wrote a song, " Now comes the
pleasant season " (p. 89), to welcome him.

This song is one of the latest we have from him.　About
a year later he wrote a short song, " I want to make a half-
sirventes of the two Kings " (p. 90), concerning a war which
threatened to break out between Richard and his old enemy
Philip Augustus.　It seems that King Alfonso VIII. of
Castile, Richard's brother-in-law, had promised to bring
an army to help him, and Bertran alludes to this promise.
Apparently the prospect of a war rejoiced him as much as
ever it had done, although he was growing old, but at the
end of this same year, 1195, he decided to give up war and
all the other delights of this world, and to end his days in a
monastery.　He chose as his retreat the Abbey of Dalon,
whither Bernart of Ventadorn had preceded him a year
before.　This Abbey was near his own castle, and he and his
family had made it many gifts.　He lived for several years

longer, perhaps till 1215, but he wrote no more songs after entering the Abbey. Perhaps he repented of having helped to stir up strife for so long, and sought to expiate his sins by spending his last years in peace and obscurity.

Bertran de Born excels among the trobadors as a writer of political satires—*sirventes*, as they were called in Provençal. The sirventes had a peculiarity of construction which distinguished it from all other Provençal lyric forms. Whereas it was a fixed rule as regards other songs that every new poem must have a new form and melody, the sirventes was written to the tune and in the form of some already existing song, in order no doubt that it might become quickly known and sung by every one. According to some, the sirventes receives its name from being the "servant" of another poem, but it is more probably so called because it is written in the service of a lord.

Bertran was usually happy in his choice of models on which to write his songs, and there is a good deal of vigour and rhythm in his lines which marks him out as a good poet as well as a master of invective. His love-songs are less beautiful than those of many other trobadors, but his two laments on the death of the "Young King" are among the very finest poems in the language.

I

A War-Song for the Count of Toulouse (1181)

The Count has asked and incited me, through Lord Raimon Luc d'Esparro, to make such a song for him that because of it a thousand shields shall be cleft, helmets and hauberks and coats of mail and doublets shall be spoilt and broken.

Now it must be made since he lets me know his words, and
I should by no means refuse since he has agreed to this
with me, for the Gascons will blame me for it, for I
hold myself under obligation to them.

At Toulouse beyond Montagut the Count will plant his
standard, in the Count's meadow near the perron, and
when he has pitched his tent we will lodge round it,
and for three nights we shall sleep on the bare ground.

And with us will have come the powers and the barons
and the most honoured company in the world, and the
most renowned, for they will be incited by money, by
the summons, and by (their own) worth.

And as soon as we have come, the fight will begin in the plain,
and the Catalans and the Aragonese shall fall thick and
fast, for their saddles shall never hold them, such great
blows and thick shall we deal them.

And it cannot be but that splinters shall fly upwards,
and that samite and silk and stuff shall be torn, cords,
tents, pikes, palisades, and tents and pitched pavilions
scattered.

The King who has lost Tarascon, and the lord of Montar-
bezo, Rogier and Bernart Ato the son, and the Count
Sir Peire help them, and the Count of Foix with Ber-
nardon and Lord Sancho, brother of the conquered
King.

Over there they think of armour, for here they will be
waited for.

I always wish that the high barons should be enraged against
each other.

II

Explanation.—Bertran de Born, as I have told you in the
other explanations, had a brother who was called Constantin
de Born, and he was a good knight at arms, but he was not
a man who troubled himself much about valour or honour,
but at all times he wished evil to Sir Bertran and well to
all those who wished evil to Sir Bertran.   And once he
took from him the castle of Autafort, which belonged to
both of them in common, and Sir Bertran recovered it and
drove him out of possession.   And that one went off to
the Viscount of Limoges and (told him) he ought to support
him against his brother ; and he supported him.   And
King Richard supported him against Sir Bertran.   And Sir
Richard was making war on Sir Ademar, the Viscount of
Limoges, and Sir Richard and Sir Ademar made war on
Sir Bertran, and laid waste his land and burnt it.   Bertran
had made the Viscount of Limoges swear allegiance to him,
and the Count of Périgord, who was named Talairan, from
whom Richard had taken away the city of Périgueux, and
he (Talairan) did not hurt him because of it, for he was lazy
and cowardly.   And Sir Richard had taken Gordon from Sir
Guilhem of Gordon, and he had promised to make alliance
with the Viscount and with Bertran de Born, and with the
other barons of Périgord and of Limousin and of Quercy,
whom Sir Richard had disinherited, wherefore Bertran
blamed him much, and for all these reasons he made this
sirventes.

I HAVE made a sirventes in which not a word is lacking, for
    it never cost me a clove of garlic ; and this is my custom,

that if I have brother or cousin, I share every egg and every penny with him, and if he then wants my share too, I turn him out of the community.

I keep all my wits carefully, although Sir Ademar and Sir Richard have given me a lot of trouble between them. For a long time they feared me, but now they have such strife that—if the King does not part them—their children will have plenty of it in their minds.

I always encourage and urge on the barons, I melt them and weld them together, for I thought to make havoc among them ; and I am a great fool to worry about them, for they are of worse workmanship than the iron of S. Leonard, wherefore whoever troubles himself about them is a fool.

Talairan neither trots nor gallops nor moves from his pen, nor does he fear lance or dart, but he lives like a Lombard. He is so stuffed with laziness that, when other people take sides, he stretches and yawns.

Guilhem de Gordon, you have put a strong clapper into your bell, and I love you, by God ! But the two Viscounts think you a fool and an idiot because of the contract, and they are eager that you should be of their brotherhood.

I am always fighting and making war and fencing and defending myself and moving about, and they lay waste my land and burn it, and make a clearing of my trees and mix chaff with my grain, and I have no enemy, brave or cowardly, who does not attack me now.

To Périgueux, only a hammer's throw from the walls, will

I come armed on Baiart, and if I find pot-bellied
Poitevins there, they shall see how my sword can cut,
for on their heads will I make a broth of brains mixed
with links of mail.

Barons, God save you and keep you and help you and aid
        you, and grant you to say to Sir Richard what the
        peacock said to the crow.

III

Explanation.—As you have heard many times, Sir Bertran
de Born and his brother Sir Constantin were always at
war with each other, and bore great ill-will to each other,
because each one wished to be lord of Autafort, their
common castle by right. And it happened that when Sir
Bertran had taken Autafort and driven Constantin and his
sons from the land, Sir Constantin went off to Sir Ademar,
the Viscount of Limoges, and to Sir Amblart, Count of
Périgord, and to Sir Talairan, Lord of Montagnac, to ask
their help and that they should aid him against his brother
Sir Bertran, who unjustly held Autafort, which was half his,
and would not give him any part of it, but unjustly disinherited him. And they helped him, and took counsel against
Sir Bertran ; for a long time they made great war on him,
and in the end they took Autafort from him. And Sir
Bertran escaped with his people, and began to besiege Autafort
with all his friends and relatives ; and it happened that Sir
Bertran sought agreement and peace with his brother, and
a great peace was made, and they became friends. But when
Sir Bertran was inside the Castle of Autafort with all his

people, he played him false, and did not keep oath or agreement with him, and took the castle from his brother with great wickedness; and this was on a Monday, when there were such signs that, according to the reason of auguries or signs, or astronomy, it was not good to begin any great undertaking. And Constantin went away to King Henry of England and to Sir Richard, the Count of Poitou, to ask for support against Sir Bertran. And King Henry, because he bore ill-will to Sir Bertran for that he was friend and counsellor to the Young King, his son, who had been at war with him, and he thought it was all Sir Bertran's fault, began to help him, he and Count Richard his son; and they made a great army and besieged Autafort, and in the end they took the castle and Sir Bertran. And when he was led into the tent before the King, he was sore afraid, but because of the words in which he reminded King Henry of the Young King, his son, the King gave him back Autafort and pardoned him, he and Count Richard, for all his evil will, as you have heard in the story which is written above the sirventes which says, "Since the fair flowery season." But when King Henry gave him back Autafort, he said, joking to Sir Bertran, "Let it be thine; thou oughtest indeed to have it by right, such great wrong didst thou to thy brother." And Sir Bertran knelt down before him and said: "My Lord, great thanks! Such a judgment pleases me well." And Sir Bertran entered into the castle, and King Henry and Count Richard returned to their own land with their people. When the other barons who were helping Constantin heard and saw that Sir Bertran still had the castle, they were much grieved and angered, and they advised Constantin to accuse Sir Bertran before King Henry, that he should support him well by right, and he did so. But Bertran showed the King the judgment that he had made—for he

had carefully had it written down—and the King laughed
and joked at it; and Sir Bertran went away to Autafort,
and Constantin had no other justice. But the barons who
were helping Constantin made great war on him for a long
time, and he on them. And as long as he lived, he would
not give up the castle to his brother, nor make peace or
truce with him; and when he was dead, the sons of Sir
Bertran made peace with Sir Constantin their uncle, and
with his sons their cousins. And for these reasons Sir Bertran
made this sirventes.

I DELAY not at all in making a sirventes, but make it without
　　any trouble at all; so subtle is my wit and my art that
　　I have advanced myself so; and I know so much magic
　　that, behold, I have escaped, for neither Count nor
　　King has injured me at all.

And since the King and Count Richard have pardoned me
　　their ill-will, never need Sir Ademar or Sir Amblart
　　or Sir Talairan make truce with me; nor will I ever
　　leave the garden of Autafort; whoever wants to may
　　make war on me for it, since it is mine by right.

When there is peace on every hand, let there be a strip of
　　war left for me. Blight his eyes who parts me from it,
　　although I may have begun it first! Peace gives me no
　　comfort; I agree with war, for I neither hold nor believe
　　any other law.

And I do not care for Monday or Tuesday, or weeks or
　　months or years, nor for April or May do I stop planning
　　how harm may come to those who do me wrong. Never
　　from me by force shall three men conquer the worth
　　of a strap.

Whoever may plough and cultivate his land, I have always
taken trouble about how I may get bolts and darts,
helmets and hauberks, horses and swords, for thus do I
please myself; and I take joy in assaults and tournaments,
in making gifts and making love.

My partner is such an insolent man that he wants my
children's possessions, and I am willing to give him some,
so easy-going am I; and then they say Bertran is
wicked because I do not give him all! But he will
come to a bad harbour, I promise you, before he makes
terms with me.

I do not care to do more good or evil about Autafort, for I
believe the judgment of my lord the King.

IV

Explanation.—At the time when the Young King had
made peace with his brother Richard, and had given up the
claim which he made on his land, as King Henry their father
wished, his father gave him a certain allowance of money
for food and necessaries; and he did not hold or possess any
land, nor did any man come to him for support or help in
war, and Sir Bertran de Born and all the other barons who
had supported him against Sir Richard were much grieved.
And the Young King went off to Normandy to fight in
tournaments and to amuse himself, and he left all these
barons at war with Sir Richard. And Sir Richard besieged
burgs and castles, and took lands, and pulled down and
burned and set fire; and the Young King was tilting and

sleeping and amusing himself; wherefore Sir Bertran made this sirventes.

I CARE not to delay longer over making a sirventes, such desire have I to say and to spread it, for I have such a new and such a great reason in the Young King, who has given up his claim on his brother Richard, since his father wishes it, so bullied is he! Since Sir Henry does not hold or command land, let him be King of the dastards!

For he acts like a dastard since he lives thus just on a paid and promised allowance. A crowned King who takes a pension from others is not much like Arnaut, the Marquis of Bellanda, or the noble Guilhelm who conquered Tor Mirmanda, so brave was he! Since he has lied to them in Poitou and reduced them to beggary, he will never be so much loved.

Never by sleeping will the King of the English gain Cumberland, nor will he conquer Ireland, or hold Anjou or Montsoreau or Candé, nor will he have the watch-tower of Poitou, nor will he be called Duke of the Norman country, nor will he be Count Palatine of Bordeaux here, or lord of the Gascons beyond Landes or of Basatz.

I want to give advice in the tune of Lady Alamanda to Sir Richard, though he does not ask for it; he need never treat his men well for fear of his brother, by no means does he do it; but he besieges and pillages them, he takes their castles and pulls down and burns on every side. And let the King tilt up there with the people of Garlande, and the other (King), his brother-in-law.

I would that Count Jaufre, who holds Bresilianda, had been
    the first-born.

For he is courteous, and would that kingdoms and duchies
    were in his command.

V

Lament on the Death of the " Young King " Henry

    If all the grief and tears and misery
    And all the sad world's wretchedness and woe
    And sorrow were united, there would be
    No fitting lamentation even so
    Made for the death of the young English King,
    Whereat the young and noble are dismayed,
    And all the world is plunged in gloom and shade,
    Deprived of joy and filled with grief and sorrow.

    Desolate, sad, and full of misery
    The courteous soldiers are, and sad also
    The trobadors and joglars, for they see
    That Death has been to them a deadly foe
    Who's taken from them the young English King,
    Compared with whom the generous were mean.
    There never will be, nor has ever been,
    In all the world such weeping and such sorrow.

    Arrogant Death, bringer of misery,
    Well may'st thou boast the world is sore distrest
    For the best knight that ever was, through thee.

Of qualities the noblest and the best
All could be found in the young English King.
Better it were, if such had been God's will,
That he should live than many rogues who fill
The hearts of noble men with grief and sorrow.

The joys of this sad life of misery
I hold as false, when love has gone away ;
All things in sorrow have their end, ah me !
And the world grows more worthless day by day.
Let all men look at the young English King,
At him who was the bravest of the brave,
And whose fair body now lies in the grave,
Whence there is dole and wretchedness and sorrow.

To Christ Who, pitying our misery,
Came to the world when it had gone astray
And suffered death from sin to set us free,
As He is just and humble, let us pray
That He will grant to the young English King
His pardon (and we shall not pray in vain),
And let him ever with the Saints remain
There where was never grief nor will be sorrow.

VI

Explanation.—At the time when Sir Richard was Count
of Poitou, before he was King, Bertran de Born was his
enemy, because Sir Bertran wished well to the Young King,
who was then at war with Sir Richard, who was his brother.
Sir Bertran had made the good Viscount of Limoges, who

was named Sir Ademar, and the Viscount of Turenne and the Viscount of Ventadorn, and the Viscount of Gimel, and the Count of Périgord and his brother, and the Count of Angoulême and his two brothers, and Count Raimon of Toulouse, and the Count of Flanders, and the Count of Barcelona, and Sir Centolh d'Astarac, a Count of Gascony, and Sir Gaston de Béarn, Count of Begora, and the Count of Dijon, take an oath against Sir Richard. And all these abandoned him and made peace without him, and broke faith with him. And Sir Ademar the Viscount of Limoges, who was most of all bound to him by love and agreement, abandoned him and made peace without him. And Sir Richard, when he knew that all these lords had abandoned Sir Bertran, came before Autafort with his army, and said and swore that he would never go away if he did not give him Autafort, and did not come at his command. Bertran, when he heard what Sir Richard had sworn, and knew he was abandoned by all those of whom you have heard, then gave him the castle and came at his command. And Count Richard received him, pardoning him and kissing him. Wherefore Bertran made this sirventes for these two reasons. And you must know that for one stanza which he made in the sirventes, which begins, "If the Count is merciful to me and not harsh," Count Richard forgave him his ill-will and restored to him his castle of Autafort, and they became true hearty friends. And Sir Bertran goes off and begins to make war on Sir Ademar, the Viscount who had abandoned him, and on the Count of Périgord, whence Bertran received great harm, and he did them great evil. And Sir Richard, when he had become king, went over the seas, and Sir Bertran remained fighting.

I AM not at all discouraged if I have lost, nor do I cease singing and rejoicing, and trying how I can recover Autafort, which I have given up to the Lord of Niort, since he wished it; and since I came before him begging for mercy, the Count, forgiving me, kept me back and kissed me; I ought to have no harm at all from that, whatever he said to me last year, for no slanderer deceives him.

Three Paladins have perjured themselves against me, and the four viscounties of Limousin; and the two effeminate Perigordians, and the three stupid Counts of Angoumois. Sir Centolh, with Gaston and all the other barons, made an agreement with me, and the Lord of Dijon with the Breton Count and Sir Raimon of Avignon, and never a single one of them kept faith with me.

A friend who does not keep faith is no better than an enemy who does me no harm. In an ancient monastery of Saint Martial many great lords swore to me on a missal: such an one pledged me his faith that he would make no treaty without me, and afterwards he kept to nothing that he had said, and it beseemed him not well at all, for he threw himself on the Count's mercy and made peace with him—this I assure you on my faith.

If the Count is merciful to me and not harsh, I will serve him very well in his affairs, and be true as silver, humble and loving; and the Count should act wisely as the sea does: when anything of value falls into it it wills that it should remain with it, and that which is no good to it it casts up on the sand. Thus it beseems a baron to pardon, and if he takes anything away, he should then give something back.

I wish to ask the Count to tell me to guard my castle or to give it to me, for always all these barons are miserly to me, for I cannot be with them without quarrelling. Now the Count can get me back without loss of dignity, and I can turn to him and serve him; and I would not do it until the desertion of Sir Ademar.

Lady of the heart miserly of promising and giving, since you will not grant me more, give me a kiss; thus you can make me rich and cure all my ills, if God and faith protect me.

Papiol, go tell my song to my lady; for love of Sir Ademar I cease to make war.

VII

Explanation.—Never for anything that Sir Bertran de Born might say in stanzas or sirventes to King Philip, or for reminders of wrong or shame that had been done or said to him, would he fight with King Richard; but Sir Richard rushed into war when he saw the weakness of King Philip, and robbed and took and burned castles, and burgs and towns, and killed and imprisoned men; wherefore all the barons, whom the peace displeased, were very glad, and Sir Bertran more than any, because he desired war more than other men, and because he believed that through his words King Richard had begun the war, wherefore he called him Yea-and-Nay, as you shall hear in the sirventes which he made.

I CANNOT resist spreading a song since Yea-and-Nay has set fire and drawn blood, for a great war makes a miserly lord generous, wherefore it pleases me well to see the pomp of the Kings, for they will need palisades, cords, and tent-pole knobs, and tents must be pitched for lodging in the open; and we shall meet by thousands and hundreds, so that men will sing of our deeds after our time.

For I would have received blows on my shield because of it and stained my white banner to red, but I abstain and go without it, because I know that Yea-and-Nay is loading a die for me; and indeed I do not possess Lusignan or Rancon that I can make war for long without wealth, but I can help my friends with my shield slung round my neck and my helmet on my head.

If King Philip had burnt a boat or drained a pond before Gisors, so that he might enter by force into the wood of Rouen and besiege it by hill and by valley, so that only a pigeon could carry letters there, then shall I know that he will wish to be like Charles, who was one of the best of his ancestors, by whom Apulia and Saxony were conquered.

War brings shame on him who is not found noble, and robs him of worth, wherefore I do not think my Yea-and-Nay will abandon Cahors and Cajarc, since he is so cunning. If the King (Henry) gives him the treasure of Chinon—he has the heart for war, and will then have the means for it. Hard work and expense are so pleasing to him that he is ever harrying friends and enemies.

Never a ship at sea when it has lost its boat and there is a storm, and it strikes on the reef and sails more swiftly than arrow from bow and rises high and then sinks low, ever endured worse things—and I will indeed tell you why—than I do through her who will not keep me, for she does not maintain day, term, or agreement; wherefore my joy, which was flourishing, is unlucky.

Go, Papiol, at once, quickly and swiftly ; be at Träinac before the feast.   Say to Sir Roger from me, and to all his relatives, that I must finish the poem for want of fresh rimes.

VIII

If I were so much lord and master of myself that I were not in love, and if love had me not in his power, I would indeed do thus much : I would let everybody know about King Philip, and what death and harm and grief it is that he is not noble, and that Ponthieu and France are degenerating.

And here Richard catches hares and lions, so that none remain in plain or wood, but he makes them keep quiet and hidden because of his power, for not a single one dares to move ; and he thinks indeed henceforward to catch great eagles with hawks and put falcons to shame with bustards.

And there King Philip chases partridges and little birds with falcons, yet men dare not tell him the truth, because little by little he is abasing himself here to Sir Richard ; for this year he has taken from him Angoulême, of which he has made himself master, and Toulouse, which he claims.

And since he is not wrathful for (the loss of) his lands, let him remember his sister and the proud husband who left her and would not have her : this insult seems to me unpleasing ; and now above all that he goes off perjuring himself, for the King of Navarre has given

him as husband to his daughter, wherefore the shame
is greater.

And if he thus loses his rights while he is young, when he is
old he will be ashamed because of it.   And the French
may never have good hope, for what men here were wont
to fear so much has been taken from them ; here towards
Poitou they care nothing for their sayings or their
demands, but laugh at them when Sir Richard and Sir
Bertran are together.

And they will come here with the spring flowers and their
pomp will be overthrown, and never will Sir Gaston
be able to help them ; but we will take from them the
Mount near Saint-Sever, and Rocafort, all that they
have taken from us, so that our torch will be finely
kindled in Poitou so that all can see this.

IX

To Conrad, Marquis of Montferrat

A Crusading Song

Now I know who has the greatest worth of all those who rose
up early ; Messer Conrad has the truest without deceit,
who is defending himself out there at Tyre against Sir
Saladin and his wicked herd.   May God help him, for
help tarries ; he alone will have the praise who alone
suffers the trouble.

Lord Conrad, I commend you to Jesus, for I should be out
at Tyre, I assure you, but I gave it up because the Counts
and Dukes and Kings and Princes delayed ; then I saw
my beauteous fair-haired lady, wherefore I became

weak; otherwise I would have been there a good year ago.

Lord Conrad, I know two Kings who delay to help you; now hear who: King Philip is one, for he fears King Richard, and Richard fears him. Now would that both of them were in the chain of Sir Saladin, since they deceive God, for they have taken the Cross and speak no word of going.

Lord Conrad, I sing all for love of you, nor do I care at all for friend or enemy, but I do it only that I may blame the Crusaders because of the journey which they have so forgotten. They do not think it angers God that they feast and amuse themselves, and you endure hunger and thirst and they delay.

Lord Conrad, the wheel goes turning in this world, but it has its end in evil, for I know few who are not always studying how they may deceive friends and strangers, but he who loses does not rejoice. Wherefore let those of whom I say they do thus know well that God records what they have said and done.

Lord Conrad, King Richard is worth so much—although when I want to I can say great harm of him—that this year he will come to you with as great a force as he can muster, so I hear say of a certainty; and King Philip will set out to sea with other Kings who shall come with such a force that we shall conquer beyond the Withered Tree.

Fair Papiol, go on your way spurring towards Savoy and towards Brindisi, and cross the sea, for I send you to King Conrad.

When you are there, be not angered; you must say to him that if I do not serve him now with my sword, I will serve him soon, if the Kings do not deceive me.

But it is true that I am dedicated to such a lady that if the journey does not please her, I do not think I shall go.

X

WILLINGLY would I make a sirventes if men were willing to hear it sung, for nobility, honour, and goodness are dead; and if any one could avenge them (on their murderers) there would be so many men killed and taken that, unless the world came to an end, water could not drown nor all the fire in the world burn so many.

And what you hear me tell in my song is not wrong or foolish, for God gives revenue and income which the understanding ought to know how to guide according to the man and his property. But there is nothing without moderation, and he who acts immoderately cannot raise his deeds high.

There are kingdoms, but no Kings; and counties, but neither Counts nor Barons; marches there are, but never a Marquis; and rich castles and fair dwellings, but the castellans are not there. And wealth is greater than ever before; there are plenty of provisions and little eating, by the fault of base miserly rich men.

You may see and find plenty of fair people and fair array, but Ogier the Dane is not there, nor do Berart and Baudoin appear; and there are plenty of combed and shaven and moustached coxcombs, but no one who knows the art of love, of holding courts, of wooing or giving.

Feeble race! Where are they who were wont to besiege castles, and who kept their court and reigned well without summons or message? And who gave rich gifts and spent much on soldiers and joglars? I may truly say, I see not a single one of them.

If King Philip, King of the French, was willing to give Sir Richard Gisors, a high place and high country, Richard ought to thank him very much. But if Philip were of my mind, Richard should not stir a foot towards harming him without opposition, and since he does not do it he lets himself be chained.

Papiol, pray hasten; tell Sir Richard from me that he is a lion, and King Philip seems to me a lamb, since he thus lets himself be disinherited.

XI

Now comes the pleasant season when our ships shall come ashore, and the gallant brave King shall come, for King Richard was never more so. Then shall we see gold and silver spent, and mangonels made and discharged, walls thrown down, towers lowered and overthrown, and the enemies chained and made prisoners.

Our barons please me not at all, who have made oaths, I know not what; for this they will be ashamed, like the wolf that is caught in the trap, when our King may be expected among us, for otherwise no one of them will be able to defend himself, but they will all say,

"No man can blame me for any ill deed, but I wish
to give myself up to you."

I love the press of bucklers covered with red and blue
colours, of ensigns and of banners of different colours.
I like tents and rich pavilions to be pitched, lances
broken, shields shattered, and shining helmets cleft,
and blows given and taken. . . .[1]

I like not the company of highway robbers or of venal women ;
sacks of sterlings and angels are hateful to me, when
they are ill-gotten. And a niggardly leader ought to
be hanged, and a rich man who wants to sell his gifts ;
and men ought not to like an avaricious woman who can
be conquered by money.

I like the custom which the lion has, that is not cruel to a
conquered thing, but is proud against pride. And the
King has not one such baron, but when they see that
his luck is down, each one strives how he may hurt
him. And you need not think that I write a word for
sale, but one ought always to fight for a noble lord.

XII

I WANT to make a half-sirventes of the two Kings, for soon
we shall see who will have more knights than the valiant
King of Castile, Lord Anfos, for I hear that he is coming
and will want soldiers. Richard will spend money by
hogsheads and gallons, and holds it happiness to spend
and give, and wants no truce, but desires war more than
sparrow-hawk desires quail.

[1] A line is lost here.

If both the Kings are noble and courageous, we shall soon
see fields strewn with pieces of helmets and shields and
swords and saddle-bows, and men cleft through their
bodies to their girdles, and we shall see horses running
wild, and many lances in side and in breast, and joy
and tears and dole and rejoicing; the loss will be great,
and the gain will be immense.

We shall soon see trumpets and drums, standards and
pennons, ensigns and white and black horses, for the
season will be good, for men will take their wealth
from the usurers; and the sumpter-mule shall never go
in safety on the highway, nor a burgher without fear,
nor any merchant who may come towards France, but
whoever will take willingly shall become rich.

But if the King comes, I have faith in God that I shall live
or shall be cut in pieces;

And if I live, it will be great good luck for me; and if I die,
a great deliverance.

XIII

Against the Rich Peasantry

It pleases me well when I see the cursed rich people in
trouble, who make war on the noble; and it pleases me
when I see them destroyed day by day, by twenties and
thirties, and when I find them in rags and begging their
bread; and if I lie, may my sweetheart lie to me.

The peasant has the manners of a swine, for seemly living
bores him, and when he gains great riches, wealth
makes him act like a fool; wherefore one should always
keep his trough empty, and spend his money, and make
him endure wind and rain.

He who does not keep a firm hand on his serf confirms him
in disloyalty, wherefore the man is a fool who does not
put him down when he sees him rise too high ; for a
peasant, when he is in safety or fortifies himself in a
strong place, has no equal in malice, for he ruins all he
comes into contact with.

One should never pity a peasant if one sees him break an
arm or a leg, or sees him in want of anything, for a
peasant, so help me God, will never help with his own
goods even one who may touch him most by pity or
compassion, wherefore his deeds should be blamed.

Base and false race, full of deceit and usury, of pride and
impudence !   Their deeds are intolerable, for they
set God and loyalty and justice at nought ; they think
to imitate Adam—God give them ill-luck !

XIV

The Joys of War

I LOVE the spring-tide of the year
When leaves and blossoms do abound,
And well it pleases me to hear
The birds that make the woods resound
With their exulting voices.
And very well it pleases me
Tents and pavilions pitched to see,
And oh, my heart rejoices
To see armed knights in panoply
Of war on meadow and on lea.

I like to see men put to flight
By scouts throughout the countryside,
I like to see, armed for the fight,
A host of men together ride;
And my delight's unbounded
When castles strong I see assailed,
And outworks smashed, whose strength has failed,
And near the walls, surrounded
By moats, and by strong stakes enrailed,
The host that has the ramparts scaled.

And well I like a noble lord
When boldly the attack he leads,
For he, whene'er he wields his sword,
Inspires his men by his brave deeds,
Their hearts with courage filling.
When tide of battle's at the flood,
Each soldier then, in fighting mood,
To follow should be willing,
For no man is accounted good
Till blows he's given and withstood.

Axes and swords and spears and darts,
Shields battered in with many a blow
We'll see when first the battle starts,
And clash of arms as foe meets foe;
The steeds of dead and dying
Wildly will rush throughout the field,
And all who wish to be revealed
As brave will e'er be trying
How best their axes they may wield,
For they would rather die than yield.

Not so much joy in sleep have I,
Eating and drinking please me less
Than hearing on all sides the cry
" At them ! " and horses riderless
Among the woodlands neighing.
And well I like to hear the call
Of " Help ! " and see the wounded fall,
Loudly for mercy praying,
And see the dead, both great and small,
Pierced by sharp spear-heads one and all.

Barons, without delaying,
Pawn every city, castle, hall,
And never cease to fight and brawl.

Papiol, make no staying,
Lord Yea-and-Nay go rouse and call,
Tell him this peace on me doth pall.

NOTES

I. "*The Count has asked and incited me.*"

Metrical form.—Stanzas of six octosyllabic lines. Rime system,
a b b a b a.

The subject of this and of all the political sirventes is given in
the introductory notes.

Stanza 1, l. 1. "The Count." Count Raimon V. of Toulouse.
"Lord Raimon Luc d'Esparro." This personage is otherwise
unknown.

Stanza 7, l. 1. "The King who has lost Tarascon." Alfonso II.,
King of Aragon. Tarascon, a town in the county of Provence,
here stands for Provence itself. Bertran exaggerates when he
says Alfonso has already lost the county.

The other persons mentioned in this stanza are all allies of
Alfonso.

II. "*I have made a sirventes.*"

Explanation.

l. 12. "King Richard." *King* is here a blunder on the part
of the writer of the explanation. Richard did not become King
till many years later.

Poem.

Metrical form.—Stanzas of seven lines, five masculine octosyllabic and two (the fifth and seventh) feminine heptasyllabic.
Rime system, a a b b aˇ b aˇ.

Stanza 2, l. 1. "Sir Ademar." Ademar V., Viscount of Limoges
(reigned 1148–1199).

"Sir Richard." The Count of Poitou, afterwards King of
England.

Stanza 3, l. 5. "The iron of Saint Leonard." Saint Leonard was invoked by prisoners as having power to break chains. In his sanctuary many broken chains were hung.

Stanza 4, l. 1. "Talairan." Elias V. Talairan, Count of Périgord (reigned 1166–1205).

l. 2. "he lives like a Lombard." The Lombards were renowned in the Middle Ages as merchants and money-lenders, but had not the reputation of being at all honest or brave. The name was therefore often used as an expression of contempt.

Stanza 5, l. 1. "Guilhem de Gordon." This nobleman was one of the "Young King's" allies in the mutiny of 1183.

l. 2. "The two Viscounts." Probably Richard and Ademar, who had expected Guilhem de Gordon to side with them in their attack on Bertran. It appears from this sirventes that he did not do so, thus, naturally, gaining Bertran's approval.

Stanza 7, l. 1. "Périgueux." This town was the capital of the county of Périgord.

l. 2. "Baiart." Bertran's horse. Perhaps it was so called after Baiart the horse of the hero Renaud de Montauban.

Tornada, l. 3. "what the peacock said to the crow." Probably an allusion to the fable of the peacocks and the jay.

III. "*I delay not at all.*"

Explanation.

The "explainer" has confused the story of the granting of Autafort to Bertran in spite of Constantin's claims with that of the taking of the castle and pardoning of Bertran after the death of the "Young King." The song alludes to the former event.

l. 40. "the sirventes which says: 'Since the fair flowery season.'" This sirventes is a satire against the King of Aragon. The story here alluded to has been quoted in the introductory notes.

Poem.

Metrical form.—Stanzas of eight lines, the first four of eight syllables each, and the remaining four of five syllables each. Rime system, a b a b c c d d.

Stanza 2, l. 2. "Sir Amblart." It is not known who this may be. According to the explanation, he was Count of Périgord, but this is clearly a mistake, as the Count's name was Elias.

"Sir Talairan." Probably Guilhem Talairan, Lord of Montagnac, younger brother of the Count of Périgord.

IV. "*I care not to delay longer.*"

Metrical form.—Stanzas of eight lines. The first five lines are decasyllabic feminine, then comes a tetrasyllabic masculine line, then another long feminine line, then a hexasyllabic masculine line. Rime system, aˇaˇaˇaˇaˇb aˇb.

Stanza 2, l. 3. "Arnaut, the Marquis of Bellanda." Arnaut de Beaulande, the hero of an old French epic.

l. 4. "Guilhelm." Guillaume d'Orange, grandson of the above. The episode here alluded to occurs in the epic "La Prise d'Orange." The tower here called Tor Mirmanda, is called Gloriete in the epic.

Stanza 4, l. 1. "the tune of Lady Alamanda." *i.e.* the song from which Bertran took the form of this sirventes. The song of Lady Alamanda is a *tenso*, or dispute, between the trobador Guiraut de Bornelh and Alamanda, the confidante of his lady. Words and music are still extant. Bertran departs from his original in one particular ; he keeps the same rimes throughout, while Guiraut and Alamanda change the feminine rimes for every two stanzas.

l. 6. "the people of Garlande." Garlande is a French barony, and the expression here means "the French people."

l. 7. "his brother-in-law." Philip Augustus of France, whose sister the "Young King" had married.

Tornada 1, l. 1. "Count Jaufre, who holds Bresilianda." Geoffrey, Duke of Brittany, the third son of Henry II. Jaufre is the Provençal form of Geoffrey. Bresilianda is Brocéliande, a forest in Brittany ; the name is here used to designate Brittany.

V. "*If all the grief and tears and misery.*"

Metrical form.—The translation observes exactly that of the original, except that the rimes of ll. 2 and 4, and ll. 6 and 7, remain unchanged throughout. Note the recurrence of the refrain words *misery* and *sorrow* at the end of the first and last lines of each stanza, and of the phrase "the young English King" in l. 5.

VI. "*I am not at all discouraged.*"

Explanation.

l. 10. "the Count of Flanders." Philip of Alsace. As he is not mentioned in the poem or in the chronicles as being in the alliance against Richard, his inclusion in the list is probably a mistake on the part of the writer of the explanation.

l. 11. "the Count of Barcelona." King Alfonso II. of Aragon had this title, but Barcelona is probably a mistake for Brittany. *Cf.* Stanza 2.

Poem.

Metrical form.—Stanzas of fifteen lines. The first eight lines are alternately of six and four syllables. Rime system, a b a b a b a b. The remaining seven lines are all of six syllables on one rime, c. The rimes change for every stanza.

Stanza 1, l. 3. "the Lord of Niort." Richard, so called from the town of Niort in Poitou. This is yet another example of Bertran's custom of using the name of a single place to designate a whole province.

Stanza 2, l. 1. "Three Paladins." The Paladins were the great men of the kingdom. It is not known to whom he refers here, but most probably he means the Dukes of Brittany and Burgundy and the Count of Toulouse, although they are alluded to later on in this stanza, as they were the most powerful noblemen in the alliance.

l. 2. "the four viscounties of Limousin." These were Limoges, Ventadorn, Torena (Turenne), and Comborn. The Viscounts were Ademar V., Ebles V., Raimon II., and Archambaut V. The last-named is called Viscount of Gimel in the explanation, from Gimel, a castle in the viscounty of Comborn.

l. 2. "the two effeminate Perigordians." The Count of Périgord and his brother.

l. 3. "the three stupid Counts of Angoumois." Guilhem V., Count of Angoulême, and his brothers Ademar and Elias.

l. 5. "the Lord of Dijon." Hugo III.. Duke of Burgundy.

l. 6. "the Breton Count." Geoffrey, Duke of Brittany.

l. 6. "Sir Raimon of Avignon." Raimon V., Count of Toulouse.

Stanza 3, l. 2. "an ancient monastery of Saint Martial." Probably that in Limoges, where the conspiracy against Richard was arranged.

Tornada 1. It is not known to which lady this tornada is addressed.

Tornada 2. "Papiol." Bertran's favourite joglar.

VII. "*I cannot resist spreading a song.*"

Metrical form.—The song is written in the form of one by Arnaut Daniel, and has eight decasyllabic lines in each stanza, which rime with the corresponding lines of the other stanzas. The rime words are mostly difficult, hence the remark in the tornada.

Stanza 1, l. 1. "Yea-and-Nay." Bertran's well-known sobriquet for Richard.

Stanza 2, l. 5. "Lusignan." A barony in Poitou. "Rancon." A barony in Limousin.

Stanza 3, l. 2. "the wood of Rouen." A deer-forest near Rouen.

l. 5. "Charles." Charlemagne. Bertran was fond of holding up the great Emperor as an example to Philip.

Stanza 4, l. 3. "Cahors and Cajarc." The former was the principal town of Quercy; the latter a castle in the same province.

l. 4. "the treasure of Chinon." Henry II. had a great treasure in the castle there.

Tornada, l. 1. "Träinac." Treignac in Limousin.

l. 2. "Sir Roger." This personage is otherwise unknown.

l. 3. "I must finish the poem for want of fresh rimes." Literally, "I find no more *omba*, or *om*, or *esta*"—these being some of the rimes chosen by Arnaut Daniel in the poem here imitated.

VIII. "*If I were so much lord and master.*"

Metrical form.—Stanzas of seven decasyllabic masculine lines. Rime system, a a b b c a c.

Stanza 3, l. 4. "he has taken from him Angoulême . . . and Toulouse." Richard had taken them, not from Philip himself, but from his vassals.

Stanza 4. Richard had promised to marry the French King's

sister Alois, but threw her over, and became betrothed to Beren-
garia, daughter of the King of Navarre.

Stanza 5, l. 7. "Sir Bertran."   Probably Bertran here alludes
to himself.

Stanza 6, l. 2. "Sir Gaston."   Gaston VI. of Béarn.

l. 4. "the Mount near Saint-Sever."   Mont de Marsan, near
the town and abbey of Saint-Sever.

l. 4. "Rocafort."   Roquefort, near Saint-Sever.

IX. "*Now I know who has the greatest worth.*"

Metrical form.—Stanzas of seven lines.   The fifth line is heptasyllabic and feminine, the others are decasyllabic and masculine.
Rime system, a b a b cˇa a.

Stanza 1, l. 2. "Messer Conrad."   Conrad, Marquis of Montferrat. *See* Introductory Notes.

Stanza 6, l. 7. "the Withered Tree."   A mythical tree said to
have existed since the beginning of the world ; to have dried up at
the time of Christ's death, and to be destined to grow green again
when a Western Prince has conquered the Holy Land.   According
to one tradition it was in Palestine, to another in Persia, and to
a third in the extreme North, the legendary "earthly Paradise."

Tornada 1. "towards Savoy and towards Brindisi."   The route
that would be taken by a traveller to the Holy Land.

X. "*Willingly would I make a sirventes.*"

Metrical form.—Eight octosyllabic masculine lines.   Rime
system, a b a b a a b b for first two stanzas.   Stanzas 3 and 4 have
rimes c c for ll. 5 and 6, and stanzas 5 and 6 have rimes d d for
these lines.   The other rimes are constant throughout.

Stanza 4, l. 2. "Ogier the Dane . . . Berart and Baudoin."
All heroes of the Charlemagne epics.

Stanza 6, l. 2. "Gisors."   The towns of Gisors and Vexins
had been the marriage portion of Philip's sister Marguerite when
she wedded the "Young King."   After the latter's death, Philip
had demanded the towns again, and this demand was the cause of
the war of 1187.   An agreement was finally made between Philip
and the old King Henry, that Philip should give up the towns in
return for 20,000 marks of silver, and shortly after King Henry's
death, Richard had promised to increase the sum by 4000 marks.

Apparently this money was never paid, for in the spring of 1191, shortly before the departure of the two Kings from Messina, where they had spent the winter, for the Holy Land, Philip seems to have given up the towns unconditionally.

Tornada. Richard was of course universally known as "Cœur de Lion," on account of his courage. We are told by the chronicler Ricardus Diviensis that the Sicilians, among whom they dwelt from September 1190 to April 1191, used to call Richard a lion and Philip a lamb; and it is possible that these nicknames had been brought to France, and that Bertran, seeing their appropriateness, adopted them in this sirventes.

XI. "*Now comes the pleasant season.*"

Metrical form.—Stanzas of eight lines, the first four masculine octosyllabic, the others feminine decasyllabic. Rime system, a b a b cˇcˇcˇcˇ.

XII. "*I want to make a half-sirventes.*"

Metrical form.—Stanzas of eight decasyllabic lines, the sixth and seventh feminine, the rest masculine. Rime system, a b a b b cˇcˇb. Stanza 1, l. 3. "Anfos." The Provençal form of Alfonso.

XIII. "*It pleases me well.*"

Metrical form.—Stanzas of eight heptasyllabic lines. Lines 4 and 7 are masculine, the rest are feminine. Rime system, aˇaˇaˇb aˇaˇb aˇ. The masculine rime remains throughout; the feminine rime changes for every stanza.

This is an example of the moral sirventes—the attack on the vices of a particular class; in this case the rich peasantry.

XIV "*I love the springtide of the year.*"

Metrical form.—The original has been exactly preserved in the translation, except that in it the rimes remain unchanged.

I have included this poem among the works of Bertran de Born, though it is not certain that he is really the author of it. It is preserved in thirteen MSS., four only of which include it under his works. In three it is attributed to Guilhem de Sant Gregori, in three to Blacasset, in two to Lanfranc Cigala, and in one to Guilhem Augier.

Songs are often attributed in the MSS. to writers other than their real author, but the strongest argument against Bertran's authorship of this song is the presence in eight MSS., namely, all but one of those which attribute it to another trobador, of a sixth stanza, addressed to a certain Lady Beatris, who is not otherwise mentioned by Bertran.

This stanza, though it is written on the same rimes as the rest of the poem, has no connection with it as regards subject, and may have been written independently (in imitation of the same model as Bertran's) and incorporated into Bertran's poem by the copyists on account of its similarity of form. One of the MSS. containing this stanza has yet another, which is certainly not part of the original poem, being found separately and anonymous in other MSS. It is possible that the copyists who put in the "Lady Beatris" stanza purposely altered the name of the author, seeing that it did not suit Bertran's style.

Let us now turn to the evidence in favour of Bertran's authorship. The tornada addressed to the joglar Papiol, bidding him carry the song to "Lord Yea-and-Nay," seems at first sight the most striking proof, but it must be confessed that this tornada is only found in two MSS., one of which attributes the poem to Bertran, the other to Blacasset. Both these MSS. were copied from the same source. It is possible that this tornada is a later addition to the poem, put in to give it the air of being the work of Bertran.

The MS. which attributes the poem to Blacasset contains also the "Lady Beatris" stanza. Two other MSS. contain a tornada which is certainly not by Bertran. The general contents and style of the poem are really more trustworthy evidence than the tornada to Papiol. Not only is the delight in war eminently characteristic of Bertran, but several phrases and expressions used here occur literally in other poems by him. All this might be accounted for by saying that the author wished to imitate Bertran, but it is hardly likely that any imitator, unless he were himself a first-rate poet, could have produced such a remarkable poem. This song, in the original, is one of the finest specimens of Provençal poetry, and surely it is more reasonable to attribute it to Bertran, one of the best of trobador poets, than to any of the other writers to whom it is ascribed, all of whom were but third-rate poets.

There is one minor point in Bertran's favour. The poem is written in the form of a song by Guiraut de Bornelh. We have seen that Bertran's sirventes "I care not to delay longer," is written in the form of Guiraut's tenso with Lady Alamanda, and we are told in one of the Provençal biographies of Bertran that "the King of Aragon called the songs of Guiraut de Bornelh the wives of Bertran de Born's sirventes"—meaning that many of his songs were written on the model of Guiraut's. This particular song has such a good swinging metre and such a lively melody that we can well imagine Bertran, who had the knack of choosing suitable models for his songs, selecting the melody and form of this work of Guiraut's for a Panegyric of War.

Arnaut Daniel

HERE we have another poet whose fame is due in part to Dante's mention of him in the *Divina Commedia*; but whereas it was Bertran de Born's political influence that interested Dante, it is simply as a poet that he speaks of Arnaut Daniel. In the twenty-sixth Canto of the *Purgatorio*, the Italian poet Guido Guinicelli thus replies to Dante's praise: "O brother, this one whom I point out to thee with my finger was a better smith of his mother-tongue. He surpassed all love-songs and moral poems,[1] and let the foolish talk who think the man of Limousin excels him. They turn their faces to hearsay more than to truth, and form their opinion thus before listening to art or reason." Dante speaks to the spirit thus pointed out and inquires his name, and the poet replies in his own tongue that he is Arnaut. The "man of Limousin"

[1] Dante's expression, "prose di romanzi," has given rise to a tradition that Arnaut Daniel wrote romances as well as lyric poems. The improbability of this theory is shown by U. A. Canello in the preface to his edition of Arnaut's works. Canello considers that Dante here uses the word "romanzo" in its Provençal sense of a didactic or moral poem, and "prosa" as a sacred song. No didactic lyrics by Arnaut have come down to us, but as he is being compared here with two exclusively lyric poets, Guido Guinicelli and Guiraut de Bornelh, both of whom wrote moral as well as amatory poems, an allusion to romances of adventure would be out of place, whereas one to moral lyrics would be quite natural.

is Guiraut de Bornelh, reputed in his own day the best of the trobadors.

Dante makes frequent mention of Arnaut in the treatise *De Vulgari Eloquentia.* His great admiration for the trobador was shared by Petrarch, who calls him " the great master of love " in the *Trionfo d'Amore,* and for more than four centuries, on the strength of the judgment of these two great poets, Arnaut Daniel was believed to be the greatest of the trobadors. His reputation was not challenged till the study of trobador literature was seriously revived more than a hundred years ago. Millot in his *Histoire littéraire des Troubadours* was the first who dared to say that he was of the opinion of " the foolish," who preferred Guiraut de Bornelh, and this is the usual opinion of critics at the present day.

The dominant characteristic of Arnaut Daniel's poetry is an extreme obscurity of thought and expression. He was the most famous and finished exponent of a class of poetry known as " close " or " obscure," which found admirers before the middle of the twelfth century. Writers of this school sought to make their meaning difficult to understand by the use of unfamiliar words and expressions, enigmatical allusions, and so forth, and increased the difficulty of their own task by choosing complicated metres and uncommon rimes for their poems. Arnaut was the inventor of a form of stanza in which no lines rime with each other, but find their rimes only in the corresponding lines of the next stanza. We have already noticed in some poems by earlier trobadors that one line of a stanza did not find its rime till the following stanza, but before Arnaut's time no one had thought of carrying this principle through a whole stanza. He carried the idea still further in the *sestina,* one of the most difficult and complicated of all fixed verse forms.

The sestina has stanzas of six lines, and the final words of
the lines of the first stanza are repeated as the final words
of the lines of all other stanzas, in a certain fixed order—
namely, the last word of the sixth line of each stanza must be
the last word of the first line of the following stanza, the
last word of the first line that of the second, of the fifth line
that of the third, of the second line that of the fourth, of
the fourth that of the fifth, and of the third that of the sixth.
A translation is given below (p. 114) of the only existing
sestina by Arnaut. This trobador sometimes combined the
device of leaving lines unrimed till the following stanza, with
that—practised by many trobadors—of making lines rime
in the middle as well as at the end. When he added harsh-
sounding words and scarce rimes to these complications, the
result was far removed from poetry, and almost unintelligible.
Here is an attempt at a translation of two stanzas of this kind.

Breeze that's bitter   makes boughs their leaves
To shed   which in the spring were green,
And sweet   beaks   of the birds above
Of song bereaves,   paired   and not paired.
Why have I e'er   or done or said   pleasure
To all ?   For her   who's set me—once high—low.
I'll soon be dead   of this, unless she save me.

Though to quit her   my heart sore grieves,[1]
Yet dread   I of her eyes the sheen
To meet.   Weak's   any other's love,
Cold it me leaves,   scared   not, but spared.

[1] This first line is not a translation of the original, which says :
" So bright was my first light (? inspiration) to choose her whose
eyes my heart dreads," &c. The exigencies of the metre compelled me to change the sense.

Her words I care	to hear instead,	treasure
More, I aver.	For I do love her so,	
From foot to head	into her power I gave me.	

This " poem " contains six stanzas and a tornada, all written on the same rimes.

The reason for Dante's high opinion of Arnaut's work must be sought for in the trobador's endeavour to avoid the simple and commonplace in form and expression, and to strive after newer and more subtle effects than those gained by the usual device of writing stanzas which were subdivided into equal parts and complete in themselves, after the manner of the old popular songs. The sestina especially aroused Dante's admiration, and he imitated this form in more than one song. Distinct traces of Arnaut's style may be found in many of his later poems. Petrarch too wrote several sestinas, and this invention of Arnaut's became popular with the Italian poets. It seems strange that Arnaut's mannerisms and obscurities should have made such an impression on Dante, but it cannot be denied that, as Canello points out, his whole style is an exaggeration of the good artistic principle of suiting form to subject—a principle which Dante always strove to adhere to. Probably Dante thought the songs of Guiraut de Bornelh too simple and easy. At the present day it is scarcely possible to institute a comparison between the works of the two trobadors, for whereas we possess eighty poems by Guiraut, there are but eighteen of Arnaut's now in existence. Some of these are so obscure and involved as to be almost unintelligible, but others, such as " When the leaves fall " and " To this tune that sounds so gaily," are comparatively simple in form and decidedly poetical in expression.

Of his life we know very little. The biography only tells us that he was nobly born and came from a castle called Ribeyrac, in the bishopric of Périgord, that he learned "letters" (*i.e.* Latin literature. He tells us himself that he had not " the art of writing"), but abandoned that study and became a joglar, that he composed " with hard rimes, wherefore his songs are not easy to understand," and that he loved a lady of Gascony, wife of Sir Guilhem de Bouvila (Bouville). It is probable that he was a friend of Bertran de Born. The warrior-poet addresses an " Arnaut the joglar " in the tornada of one of his poems, and Arnaut addresses " Bertran " in one of his. The " Desirat " addressed in the sestina is considered by some commentators to be Bertran. According to an amusing story told in one version of the biography, Arnaut frequented the court of Richard Cœur de Lion, and very likely it was there that he met Bertran. At King Richard's court, we are told, " another joglar told him how he composed in more difficult rimes than he (Arnaut) did. Arnaut thought this a mockery. And each one gave his palfrey as a pledge to the King that the other would not do it. And the King shut each of them into a room. And Sir Arnaut, for the anger he had about it, had not the power to string two words together. The joglar made his song easily and quickly. And they had but the space of ten days. And they were to be judged by the King. At the end of five days the joglar asked Sir Arnaut if he had finished, and Sir Arnaut replied that he had, three days before—and he had not even thought of it. The joglar sang his song all night that he might know it well, and Sir Arnaut thought how he could mock him, until it happened one night that the joglar was singing, and Sir Arnaut had remembered every word, and the music too. And when they were before the King Sir Arnaut said that he wished to sing his song, and he began very well the song that the joglar had made. And the joglar when he heard it looked him in the face and said that *he* had made it. And the King said, 'How could that be?' And the joglar prayed the King to discover the truth about it, and the King asked Sir Arnaut how it had come about. And Sir Arnaut told him all as to how it had come about. And the King had great joy thereby, and held it all a great jest, and the wagers were restored, and he had fine gifts given to both. And the song was given to Sir Arnaut Daniel, which says: 'I never had Love in my power.'"

It is impossible to assign an exact date to any of Arnaut's poems, except one, which must have been written in 1181, but his supposed friendship with Bertran de Born, and the fact that his style was well known and much imitated before the year 1200, have led critics to fix his period of literary activity between the dates 1180 and 1200. Canello thinks that his songs were addressed to several different ladies. One was an Aragonese, perhaps named Laura, as Arnaut plays on the words *l'aura* (the air) in songs written for her. Another was a Gascon lady of high degree, whom he calls "Better than Good." However, as he observed the rules of discretion very strictly, and as we know practically nothing of his life, it is impossible to guess the identity of his ladies.

I

WHEN the leaves fall from the highest tree-tops and the cold grows proud, so that the wild vine and the osier are withered, I see that the wood no longer echoes with the sweet refrains, but I am eminent in love, whoever tears himself from it.

All things freeze, but I cannot grow cold, for a new love makes my heart grow verdant again; I ought not to

shiver, for love covers and hides me and makes me keep
my value and leads me.

A good thing is life if joy sustains it, for some cry out against
it who are by no means so fortunate. I cannot complain of anything in my lot, for by my faith my portion
is of the best.

I cannot blame anything with regard to love, for the nobility
of others I regard as worthless. I cannot compare my
lady with her equal, for there is no one who is not
second to her.

I do not wish that my heart should turn to another love,
so that I rob myself of it and she turns her head elsewhere ; I do not fear that ever he of Pontremoli has a
fairer one than her, or one who resembles her.

She whose friend I am is by no means cruel ; a fairer one
does not live this side of Savoy ; she pleases me so well
that I have more joy in her than Paris, the Trojan, had
in Helen.

She who keeps me joyful seems so fair, that her lovely face
conquers thirty of the fairest. Indeed, then it is right
that she should hear my song, for she is so noble and
well dowered with great honour.

Go, song, present thyself before her, for were it not for her,
Arnaut would not have troubled to write thee.

II

To this tune that sounds so gaily
Words I fashion of the rarest ;
True and certain will they be

When my file has shaped them neatly;
Love makes smooth and gilds full fairly
This my song, inspired by one
Who is noble altogether.

Better, purer grow I daily,
Seeing her who is the fairest,
This I tell you openly.
Head to foot I'm hers completely
And though cold winds blow not rarely,
My heart's love, like summer sun,
Keeps me warm in wintry weather.

Thousand masses I've attended,
Lights of wax and oil I'm burning,
That God may to pity move
Her 'gainst whom I can't protect me;
When I see her golden tresses
And her figure fair and slim,
Nought on earth so much I treasure.

My heart's love on her's expended
And I ever fear her spurning,
So that love my loss may prove.
In a flood of love she's wrecked me
Which, ne'er ebbing, still me blesses,
I obey her every whim,
Write her songs in bounteous measure.

Emperor I would not make me,
Nor the Papacy desire,
If from her I had to part
For whose sake my heart is breaking.

If to kiss me soon she pleases
Not, 'twill kill me, I declare,
And her soul to hell deliver.

Ne'er from loving will I take me
Though I suffer torment dire,
And she never cheers my heart.
When a lover toils at making
Verse, all other toil mere ease is.
He of Monclin did not care
More for his belov'd a stiver.

I'm Arnaut who hoards the breezes,
With the ox I hunt the hare,
Swim against the rising river.

III

I NEVER had Love in my power, but he always has me in his, and makes me sad, joyful, wise and foolish, as one who never turns against him, for he who loves well does not defend himself; for Love commands that one should serve and flatter him, wherefore I wait patiently for a good share when it shall be given to me.

If I say little, I keep much in my heart, for fear makes me keep it quiet; the tongue feigns, but the heart desires that in which, grieving, it delights; for it languishes but does not complain, for in all the land engirdled by the sea there is none so fair as the elect lady whom I long for.

I know her value to be so true and certain that I cannot turn elsewhere; it is for this that my heart aches, that

when the sun sets and rises I dare not say who enflames
me ; my heart burns and my eyes feast on her, for I am
only able to see her—that is what keeps me alive.

He is a fool who, by vain talking, seeks to turn his joy to
sorrow, for slanderers—whom God confound—have by
no means flattering tongues, one gives advice and
another shouts, wherefore Love is driven away, however great it might have been. But I defend myself by feigning from their gossip, and love without
mistakes.

Therefore she keeps me rejoicing and well with a pleasure
by which she has consoled me, but it shall never pass
my lips for fear that she might be angry with me, for
still I feel the flame of Love which tells me not to
proclaim my heart, and I obey him, often fearing,
since I see many loves ruined by gossip.

I would have made many other easy and simple songs if
she who gives me joy and takes it from me had helped
me ; for now I am happy and now I change, for I am
bound to her will. My heart asks nothing from her,
nor does it evade her, but freely I dedicate it to her,
so that if she forgets me, mercy is perished.

Kind song, tell Better-than-Good that Arnaut does not
forget.

IV

Sestina

Longing that my heart doth enter
Cannot uprooted be by beak or nail
Of slanderer, who by lies ruins his soul.

Since I dare not beat him with twig or rod,
At least in secret, where I have no uncle,
I will have joy in orchard or in room.

And when I recall the room
Where to my grief I know no man can enter,
To me are all more than brother or uncle ;
In every limb I quake, even to the nail,
Just as a child does when it sees the rod,
So fear I she regards too much her soul.

There in body, not in soul,
I'd be, had she concealed me in her room !
For more it hurts my soul than blows of rod
That where she is her servant cannot enter.
I shall be to her even as flesh and nail,
And warning will not heed from friend or uncle.

Not the sister of my uncle
Loved I so much or more, upon my soul !
For close as is the finger to the nail,
If she so pleased, would I be to her room,
And love, which now within my heart doth enter,
Can bend me as a strong man a weak rod.

Since first flourished the dry rod,
Or nephew from Sir Adam sprang, or uncle,
Such faithful love as in my heart doth enter
Ne'er was, I think, in body or in soul.
Where'er she be, outdoors or in her room,
I part no more from her than length of nail.

I am held as with a nail
Fastened to her as bark is to the rod ;
To me of joy she's palace, tower and room ;
I do not love so much brother or uncle,
And double joy in Heaven 'twill give my soul
If ever man for true love there doth enter.

Now Arnaut sends his song of nail and uncle
By leave of her whose rod doth rule his soul,
To Desirat, in whose room worth doth enter.

V

Now I see red, green, blue, gold, white
Gardens, plains, shores, hillocks and vales,
And the birds' voices morn and eve
Sing sweetly many a trill and turn.
This puts it in my heart to deck my song
With such a flower whose seed is joy, and love
Its fruit, and its scent sweet as oleander.

Love sets my pensive heart alight,
And fond desire, but nothing ails
Me, for 'tis sweet for this to grieve,
And soft's the flame, howe'er it burn.
For Love asks that his servants should be strong,
Forgiving, grateful, true, and doth approve
The humble, and doth banish pride and slander.

To change me time nor space has might
And neither good nor ill avails
—And if in this I you deceive,
May the fair one to me be stern

For whom asleep or waking e'er I long.
I would not, prizing her all else above,
Lose her to gain the power of Alexander.

I'd fain once more her cook be hight,
Such joy with great delight one hails,
Twenty years more then I believe
I'd live, such joy from her I earn.
Bah ! I'm a fool ! What more then should belong
To me (to other loves I'll never rove) ?
Seek I the wealth of Tigris or Meander ?

Without her I find all delight
Is dull, I heed not others' tales,
My thoughts and words can never leave
Her, and for her alone I yearn,
For nothing else I want from all the throng
Of pleasures—she of joy is treasure-trove ;
I'd see her in my heart were I in Flanders.

It seems a year from morn to night,
All pleasure to amuse me fails,
It grieves me that I can't achieve
The art of shortening time to learn.
True lovers pine when made to wait too long.
Oh Sun and Moon, too slowly do you move,
I grieve that you do not more quickly wander.

To her who owns me go, my song, along ;
Her merits Arnaut can't describe or prove,
For it would need talent than his far grander.

NOTES

I. " *When the leaves fall.*"

Metrical form.—The stanzas have eight lines, feminine lines of four syllables alternating with masculine lines of six. Rime system, aˇb aˇb aˇb aˇb. The rimes change for every stanza.

The simplicity of form and thought are not at all characteristic of Arnaut Daniel.

Stanza 2. " All things freeze." A thought similar to that expressed here may be found in Bernart of Ventadorn's song, " Such delight has come to me." Arnaut may have borrowed the idea from this song. He uses it again in " To this tune that sounds so gaily."

Stanza 5, l. 3. "he of Pontremoli." Very likely this alludes to the Marquis Albert of Malaspina, an Italian trobador noble. He was not lord of Pontremoli, but possessed a castle near by.

Stanza 6, l. 3. " Paris, the Trojan." It need hardly be said that Arnaut derived his knowledge of Paris and Helen from the *Roman de Troie*, not from Homer.

II. " *To this tune that sounds so gaily.*"

Metrical form.—This song is an example of Arnaut's practice of riming his lines from stanza to stanza only. In the original, the same rimes are kept up throughout the poem ; in the translation I have changed them for every two stanzas. The translation reproduces the metrical form of the original in every other particular.

Stanza 6, ll. 6 and 7. " He of Monclin," &c. These real or legendary lovers have not been identified. Possibly they are the hero and heroine of a romance that is now lost.

Tornada.—In the original there are plays upon words that cannot be preserved in translation. *L'aura* (the breeze) may stand for *Laura*, Arnaut's lady, and *lebre* (hare) for *l'Ebre*, the river

Ebro. The conceits of "collecting the breezes" and "hunting the hare with the ox," appear to have greatly pleased Petrarch, who uses them in two poems, a sonnet and a sestina. It is even possible that the name of Petrarch's lady, "Laura," is taken from these very lines of Arnaut. It is by no means certain that Laura was the real name of Petrarch's lady; it may very possibly have been only a pseudonym, such as the trobadors used. Petrarch is continually playing on the words *Laura* and *l'aura*, and it is not unlikely that, admiring Arnaut as he did, he borrowed the whole idea from him.

III. "*I never had Love in my power.*"

Metrical form.—There are eleven lines in each stanza; the first three are octosyllabic masculine, the fourth and fifth heptasyllabic feminine, the sixth tetrasyllabic feminine, the seventh hexasyllabic feminine, the eighth tetrasyllabic masculine, the ninth dissyllabic masculine, the tenth tetrasyllabic feminine, and the eleventh pentasyllabic feminine. The first five lines find their rimes only in the corresponding lines of the other stanzas; the rime system of the last six lines is aˇaˇ, b b, cˇcˇ. The same rimes are kept throughout.

In spite of the complicated structure of the stanza, this is one of Arnaut's simplest songs. It appears from the sixth stanza that Arnaut himself considered the song "easy and simple." According to the story of the wager at King Richard's court, the song was written by the joglar who was Arnaut's rival, but there is no real reason for supposing that it is not Arnaut's own work.

IV. *Sestina.*

Metrical form.—The structure of the sestina has been explained in the introductory notes to Arnaut's works. The form of the original has been preserved in the translation, and the final words *enter, nail, soul, rod, uncle, room* are the same. The translation is almost literal, and if it seems nonsense in places, it is none the less like the original for that. It was natural for Arnaut to choose unpromising words such as *nail* and *uncle* for his end words, as it can have been no easy task to bring them into every stanza of a love-song.

Stanza 5, l. 1. "Since first flourished the dry rod." It is not certain to what this passage refers. It may allude to Aaron's rod which flourished in the Tabernacle; or, more probably, to the Tree of Knowledge, which withered at the time of the Fall of Man, but gave the seed from which was made the wood of the Cross; or to the Blessed Virgin, who is often compared with Aaron's rod. If this last interpretation be correct, the lines would mean: Never in the time of the New Testament (Saint Mary) or of the Old (Adam and his race).

Tornada. "Desirat" may be Bertran de Born, or some other patron of Arnaut's, or a lady who was the confidante of his beloved.

"V. "*Now I see red, green, blue, gold, white.*"

Metrical form.—That of the original has been exactly preserved in the translation.

Stanza 4, l. 1. "I'd fain once more her cook be hight." It is quite possible that Arnaut had indeed cooked his lady's dinner. It was part of a joglar's trade to carry about news of every description, and it is not at all unlikely that he occasionally brought new culinary recipes from one castle to another.

l. 7. "The wealth of Tigris or Meander." Arnaut may derive his idea of the wealth of the river Tigris from the story that its source is in the terrestrial Paradise, or from the fact that it runs through the fertile land of Mesopotamia. The richness of the soil of the river Meander is vouched for by Pliny and Ovid.

Guiraut de ornelh

WE are told little more of Guiraut de Bornelh's life than of Arnaut Daniel's. In two MSS. short "explanations" are given of a few of his songs, but they are no more trustworthy than those prefixed to the sirventes of Bertran de Born. The biography itself tells none of the events of his life, but succeeds in giving a picture of the poet exactly like what, to judge from his songs, one may imagine him to have been.

"Guiraut de Bornelh was of Limousin, of the neighbourhood of Essiduoill, of a rich castle belonging to the Viscount of Limoges. And he was a man of low condition, but well versed in letters, and of natural talent. And he was a better trobador than any of those who had been before him, or who came after him—wherefore he was called Master of the Trobadors, and is still, by all those who understand subtle and well-turned sayings of love or of wit. He was greatly honoured by men of worth and understanding, and by good ladies who understood his lofty sayings and his songs. And his way of life was such, that all the winter he stayed at school and studied letters, and all the summer he went about from court to court, and took two singers who sang his

songs.   He never wanted a wife, but all he gained he gave to
his poor relations and to the church of the town where he
was born, which church was called, and still is, Saint Gervais."

Guiraut de Bornelh took his art more seriously than the
other trobadors took theirs.   The schools where he studied
were, no doubt, those connected with religious houses,
where classical literature was taught; he learned the art of
verse-making from his elder contemporaries.   The greater
number of his poems are love-songs, and while reading these
one feels instinctively that he took more interest in the
form of the songs than in the ladies to whom they were
addressed; that he chose a lady to woo in order that he might
have a subject for his songs, not that he wrote his songs
simply to please the lady.   There is more spontaneity and
sincerity in his moral sirventes, but great carefulness of form
and expression characterises almost all his poetry.   For a
short time he patronised the " obscure manner," but he
soon declared himself in favour of the style that could be
understood by every one.   It would seem as if he had always
preferred to write simply, but that the influence of some of
the early exponents of the obscure manner had caused him
to try his hand at writing in that style soon after he had
started on his literary career.   We possess a *tenso* in which
he discusses the relative merits of the two styles with a certain
Linhaure, the latter praising the difficult, and Guiraut the
clear manner.   It is supposed that this Linhaure is identical
with the trobador Raimbaut d'Aurenga, one of the first
exponents of the obscure style.   In one poem Guiraut re-
counts his decision that he will adopt the clear manner, and
alludes to a " well-instructed man " who had tried to con-
vince him that the dark manner was superior.   Ad. Kolsen
(*Guiraut von Bornelh*) considers that this " well-instructed
man " is Linhaure—*i.e.* Raimbaut d'Aurenga, and that it

was this poem that led Raimbaut to challenge Guiraut to the above-mentioned tenso. Raimbaut d'Aurenga was a nobleman who, besides being himself a trobador, patronised other poets, and we can tell from various allusions to "Linhaure" in Guiraut's poems, and especially from the Lament on his death (where he is called Ignaure), that he was his patron and friend. It is therefore not unnatural that the younger poet should have been influenced by a trobador whose art was much esteemed, and to whom he was bound by ties of friendship and of gratitude.

Guiraut's period of literary activity was a long one, extending, as far as we can gather from the allusions of other trobadors and from his own mention of different historical events, from about 1165 till 1200, or even later. Kolsen supposes that he was born about 1138. His first love affair was with a Gascon lady whom he calls Escaruenha in one of his songs. Some account of it is given in the "explanations" of two of his works. Here the lady is called Alamanda, but probably the writer of the explanations confused her with her waiting-woman.

"Guiraut de Bornelh," we are told, "loved a lady of Gascony who was called lady Alamanda of Estanc; she was a lady much prized for wit and merit and beauty, and she tolerated the prayers and the love of Sir Guiraut because he advanced her honour, and because he made good songs of her, in which she much delighted, for she understood them well. A long time he adored her, and she, with fair speeches and fair honourings and fair promises, courteously held him off, and never loved him or gave him any gift save one of her gloves, by reason of which he lived a long time gay and joyous, and then had great grief when he had lost it; for my lady Alamanda, when she saw that he supplicated her much for her love, and knew he had lost the glove,

grew angry about the glove, saying he had kept it ill, and
that she would give him no joy or pleasure and no more love,
and that she would take back what she had promised him,
for she saw well that he was very far gone away from her
command. When Guiraut heard the new blame and the
dismissal which the lady gave him, he was much grieved
and very sad, and came to a waiting-woman whom she had,
who was called Alamanda like the lady. The maiden was
very wise and courteous, and well understood song-making
and love, and Guiraut told her what the lady had said to
him, and asked counsel of the maiden as to what he should
do, and said, ' If I ask counsel of you, fair friend Alamanda.' "

This is the song which Bertran de Born chose as the
model for his sirventes, " I care not to delay longer."
Opinions are divided as to whether it is a genuine tenso, or
entirely the work of Guiraut, who was fond of writing in
dialogue form. The waiting-woman Alamanda promises
in the song to try and obtain his lady's forgiveness for
Guiraut ; but she was unsuccessful, for, according to another
explanation, " Guiraut could not do or say anything that
could bring him back to the good graces of my lady Alamanda, for she was very treacherous to him because she
wanted to be rid of him, wherefore she made the excuse
of the glove. So Guiraut, though it grieved him, left her,
and you must know that my lady Alamanda did not dismiss
him only because of the glove, although she made it the
motive, for she did it so that she might take for her lover
one by reason of whom she was much blamed, for he was
a very base and wicked man. So Guiraut de Bornelh remained very sad and grieved for a long time because of his
loss and her blame."

Kolsen thinks that he broke with his lady in the spring of

1168. At the end of the same year he went to the court of King Alfonso II. of Aragon, and stayed there some time. It is not possible to trace his career during the following years, but according to the explanation of the song, " I cannot help turning my tongue " (p. 137), he took part in the Third Crusade. The capture of Acre, at which he is said to have been present, took place on July 13, 1191, so Guiraut must have left the Holy Land in the spring of 1192. The visit that he paid to the court of King Alfonso VIII. of Castile, which is mentioned in the sirventes, " The sweet song of a bird " (p. 140), and in its explanation, probably took place some years later, as it seems likely that the King of Navarre, who had the poet robbed, was Sancho the Strong (reigned 1194–1234), who had the reputation of being a robber. A sirventes, usually supposed to be the last he wrote, has the following explanation :—

" Guiraut de Bornelh, when Gui the Viscount of Limoges had had his house robbed of his books and of all his possessions, and when he saw that nobility was fled, and joy asleep, and wooing dead, and prowess given up, and courtesy lost, and good-breeding turned to rudeness, and that deceit had entered into both sides, into ladies and into their lovers, wished to take pains to recover solace and joy and merit, and he made that song which says, ' To reawaken joy, which has fallen fast asleep.' "

Gui of Limoges was the son and successor of Ademar V. He captured the castle of Essiduoill in the year 1211, and it may be supposed that this was the occasion of the plundering of Guiraut's house, if that ever took place. Kolsen points out that the explanation does not fit the poem, in which Guiraut expressly says that his little house had never been invaded by robbers, and believes that none of Guiraut's poems were written later than 1200, as he is alluded to as a

" past " trobador in a satire by the Monk of Montaudon dating from that year. It is to be hoped that the explanation of the sirventes, " To reawaken joy," is merely a fabrication, for it is melancholy to think of the trobador being robbed in his old age of his books.

Guiraut's many moral sirventes led Dante to call him a " poet of rectitude " in a certain passage in the treatise *De Vulgari Eloquentia,* where he speaks of the three subjects that have been treated by poets in the vulgar tongue, namely, " courage in arms, ardency of love, and direction of the will." Of Provençal poets he mentions Bertran de Born as having sung of arms, Arnaut Daniel of love, and Guiraut de Bornelh of rectitude. Though he set Arnaut at the head of Provençal trobadors, Dante nevertheless greatly admired the works of Guiraut, and makes frequent mention of them in the *De Vulgari Eloquentia.* It would appear from the passage just alluded to that he thought more of his sirventes than of his love-songs, and this is the general opinion as to Guiraut's works at the present day. In his satires he combines sincerity and warmth of feeling with a certain dignity and restraint which are lacking in the satirical poetry of most of the trobadors who wrote on social and political subjects. Most of his love-songs, on the contrary, are uninspired. His metrical forms are often elaborate and effective, his language is careful and polished, his ideas are sometimes original, yet his poetry is for the most part without the charm of Bernart of Ventadorn's or Peire Vidal's.

There is, however, one song by Guiraut that cannot be classed with the rest of his love poetry—namely, his *Alba* or dawn song. The song describing the parting of lovers at daybreak is of very ancient popular origin. The idea was borrowed by the trobadors, many of whom have left very fine Albas. Guiraut's is one of the most beautiful examples of the *genre* that have come down to us. Here the poet really seems to lose himself in his subject. The metre and language he uses are of a simplicity quite unusual with him, but they fit the subject, and the poem is one of the greatest glories of Provençal literature. The music of this Alba, one of the only four existing melodies by Guiraut, is as beautiful as the words are.

I

Now I have joy, remembering the love
That keeps my heart firm in fidelity ;
For lately in a garden I did rove,
Where flowers grew and birds sang merrily.
And while I lingered in that garden fair,
Appeared the beauteous lily to me there,
And took my eyes and stole my heart from me,
So that ne'er since have I remembered aught
Save her who has my love and all my thought.

'Tis she for whom I sing and weep alway,
For she awakens true and pure desire ;
Often I sigh and supplicate and pray
Where first her beauty set my heart afire.
The flower of ladies, whom I love and prize,
Is she who's won me in such gracious wise,
Sweet, humble, good, and nobly born is she,
Her deeds are good, her converse gives delight,
Courteous she is to me in all men's sight.

Full rich I'd be, dared I her praise to tell—
All men would love to hear it—but I fear
That slanderers, cruel and base and fell,

And beyond measure false, my song might hear;
And, since they hate to see another glad,
That they would seek to know what joy I had.
But if one of her kin I chance to see,
I'll kiss him till my mouth can kiss no more,
All for her sake whom I do so adore.

Ne'er for love's sake or mine may you forbear,
False slanderers compact of wickedness,
To ask her race, and what she is, and where,
If far or near, for ne'er through me you'll guess.
Sooner than speak a word of it I'd die,
E'en to my friends concerning this I'd lie;
For no man lives who ever can be free
From foolish neighbours' evil questioning,
E'en to one's kin one cannot trust a thing. ·

Now will the scoffers, when they see me, say:
" Ah, childish one, how foolishly he stares,
And in his pride and greatness turns away ! "
For e'en at a great fair no other cares
Have I save but for her in whom my heart
Is fixed, and e'er my eyes look toward that part
Wherein she dwells, and my thought speaks to me
Ever of her whom my true heart holds dear,
For he loves not who does not make it clear.

II

HONOUR and love and cherishing,
Obedience too and humbleness,
Long begging and long friendliness
And long hope and long suffering

Would make me live in joy and rest
If with a good lord I were blest,
But since I neither change nor stray,
Love wills not that I should be gay.

And yet my knowledge and my sense,
My speaking and my nature kind,
My hope, my constancy of mind,
My fear and all my reticence,
—These would have gained me true love e'er,
Had I but sought my good elsewhere,
But she who keeps me in such woe
Nor lets me love, nor lets me go.

And if my homage she'd receive,
My wooing and my service true—
The sleepless nights I have been through,
The grief I bear from morn till eve,
Could never take me from her sight ;
I'd be a slave unto delight,
All burdens I would gladly bear
And for my heart's grief I'd not care.

Why do I know that now indeed
Life is worth less than death to me ?
—Since it lacks joy and gaiety,
And since love fails me in my need.
Why do I weep, lament and sigh ?
Because no help from joy have I ;
For no man ever loved so much,
Although my love I may not touch.

An ardent longing fights me now,
Excess of love and long desire;
Foolhardiness makes me aspire,
And foolishness, to gain somehow
What is not fitting to my state;
And if my wish is all too great,
Evil my mind may seem and vain,
But true and faithful I remain.

For my perception and my thought
And my belief and reason's light
Have taught me that no other might,
No other riches, honour, naught
Can give me so much wealth as she
Who makes me live in misery,
For while I languish and I pine
I hope she will to me incline.

Most noble lady, as I see,
Your honour and nobility
Rise ever and more brightly shine
—And faithful is this heart of mine.

III

But why is it, God help me, that now, when I think to sing,
    I weep?   Could it be through love, that has conquered
    and vanquished me?   And does not joy come to me
    through love?—Yes, indeed!   Then wherefore am I
    sad, and what makes me languish?   What, can I
    not tell?
For thus has it happened to me full soon that I have lost
    my worth, and amusement has no pleasure for me.

Did more ever happen to lover ?   Am I a lover ?—No !
And do I leave her whom I always love and wish
for and desire more strongly and more deeply ?—No !
Am I a lover ?—If I may be endured !

For now—for I have only wished—I hold myself a true
lover ; as I pray to God, I am a true lover, and I do
not move my heart, nor turn it aside from loving her
for whose sake I am joyful. I fear very little that I
shall make mistakes, so wherefore do I lament and
sigh ?

—Because I have seen clearly that love is of no use to me,
nor helps me.—Of no use ?   And I love the dearest in
the world ! Has it not been of great use ?—By no
means ! I say rather that it betrays me, for it gave
me sorrow and trouble, and made me desire that which
cannot come to me.

—And how ?   Have I not received plenty of good and
honour from the hands of " My Commander " ?—Yes,
but they have kept back more !—And what ? An
agreement, which she broke who caused my sorrow,
and will make me die if I may not devote myself to her.

Does she desire no longer what once pleased her ?—I know
not ; I deserve better. I suffer as a man does who
when most oppressed desires more salvation ! Sir
Antic, does it not seem a trouble to you ? Say Yes,
for if she ever kisses me I can safely assure you that she
can kill me or cure me.

But a complaint has increased my woe, which the people of
Urgel make among themselves, whereby most of them

will be killed and ruined ; for the Countess, with whom joy and wisdom and true worth are born, thinks to leave there, if they will consent to it.

I shall indeed hold them all wicked if they let her go out, and the King, if he consents to it.

IV

Lament on the Death of " Ignaure "

If ever I had joy or pleasure, now am I sorrowful and despairing for ever more ; for my fate does not suffer me ever to recover joy, which always flees and goes from me ; for now the sorrow comes back to me which makes me grieve on both sides.

For I was born in such an hour that it does not please God that any of my good and trusty friends should live as long as other men. Thus it happens to me with my Ignaure, whom I have not ; since My-Joy failed me first, in whom my sorrow began.

And I was a little consoled, as a man distressed may be, because you, Ignaure, loved me ; but now I shall be disconsolate since I shall not see you, and nevermore shall salutations and courteous messengers come to me from there whence all joy is wont to come.

Ah, fair, well-taught friend, simple with fools and prudent and wise with the intelligent ! For your sake I despise April and May and the sweet gay season ; nor shall I ever rejoice again, nor shall I sing willingly, but I cannot fittingly lament you otherwise.

Ah, such fair learning as you had, to whom will you leave

it ?   Will your equal ever be found ?   For I never saw
and never shall see, however far I go, so many fine
enterprises undertaken by one single man, nor can one
say that, as a knight, Oliver was worth so much.

Now is fair folly dead, and games of dice, and gifts and wooing
are forgotten ;   through you nobility is lost and
lessened ; as far as beyond Velay many good men will
become wicked because of it, to whom you were a guide
and a companion, as one well skilled in good deeds.

By your beautiful song-making, by your goodness, your
merit, your knowledge, your nobility, those who fared
most miserably could become joyful.   Never can I tell
many of your good deeds, for even good Master Berenguier would seem a liar if he did so.

In you nobility and chivalry are dead, and generosity, good
deeds, fair speech, and good joy ; wherefore, by my
faith, I shall never believe that—if justice is done—
God will not receive you first of all into His holy true
joy, since He gave you without stint so many fair gifts.

Now do they say that because of you Provence abstains from
splendid deeds, for there is no one so fit to do them.

My Above-all, if my heart were steel, it would have to break
to pieces.

V

CRUSADING SONG

I TURN to the honour of God in my song, which I had parted
from and left, and the calls and cries of birds do not
turn me from it, nor the leaves of the garden ; but I
rejoice not at all while singing, but rather I am troubled

and grieved, for in many writings I learn and see that sin conquers, wherefore faith fails and iniquity rises.

And I consider, marvelling greatly, how the world has gone to sleep, and how thoroughly the root withers and evil strives and mounts upward ; for now men hardly heed or care if God is shamed or outraged, for Syria remains in peace to the Arabians, the lawless traitors, and here the Powers quarrel among themselves.

And yet it is not at all likely, since God has fallen into such distress, that a man valiant in arms and courageous may ever turn back from before there without shame ; but he who will have received great blows from the sword of another, and struck them with his own, will be welcomed and will think himself paid by his King, for He is by no means at a loss how to give.

And since the Holy Spirit gives strength of heart and will, and parts it—that one may not be shamed thereby— from the devil who is full of deceit, those who shall go with God avoid growing haughty on account of their strength, for scarcely have you ever seen great prudence come from a great confusion of changeable wills, or from many sides.

But since we all follow one leadership and each one wishes to be approved, let him who can do most be most energetic ; for thus they may know that they shall conquer, and help those who do not go there, wherefore God may be better served ; but He says this : Let each man renounce that which pleases him most in the world, and follow Him destitute, for He came here despoiled of all things.

Ah, wretched people ! What will they say when He shall

remember their forgetfulness, and shall want an account of the little things from those who will not help Him now ? You shall see indeed that they shall 've reckoning of all that they may have governed here, and never, by the faith I owe to you, shall their guides, who will have guided them ill, give them comfort or joy.

You must know indeed that I am troubled by the harm, but I am amazed at the shame, that the ill-clad deceivers who have neither God nor law, nor anything good, should do to us as they do, for they have ill-treated us vilely, for you never heard in such wise since the time that God was born, so great a danger that was so lightly endured.

Yet I am regaining happiness which had left and departed from me, and my song is finished in joy which was begun in weeping, since I hear that the armies are going and the help of the Kings is promised ; Soldan or Emir will be ill-treated, I assure you, when they shall come, if they have not gone far from them.

And Count Richard is well equipped, and near his men ; whomever it may annoy, such a matter pleases me, for it is very great, and may God be praised for it.

VI

Explanation.—Guiraut de Bornelh crossed the sea with King Richard and with the Viscount of Limoges, who was called Sir Ademar, and he was at the siege of Acre. And when the city was taken by them, and all the barons returned thence, Guiraut de Bornelh went away to the good Prince of Antioch, who was a very noble man. He was much honoured by him and served, and he remained with him a whole winter, waiting for the passage that was to be made at Eastertide. And being with him, he dreamed a dream, which you shall hear, in that song which says : " I cannot help turning my tongue."

I CANNOT help turning my tongue to the aching of my tooth, and my heart to the spring flowers, when I see the twigs blossoming and the little birds are singing for love of each other in the coppice, and though I may be troubled and seized by misfortune, when I hear songs and see gardens and meadows, I live again and grow joyful.

For I take no trouble about other work, save singing and rejoicing, for one night at Eastertide I dreamed such a dream as made me rejoice, of a young sparrow-hawk which sat on my wrist, and though it seemed docile, I never saw one so wild, but afterwards it became tractable and tame, and trained for good casts.

I told the dream to my lord, as one ought to tell it to one's friend, and he expounded it to me wholly of love, and told me that I could not fail, after having taken great trouble about it, to gain in peace a sweetheart of higher lineage, whose like no man of my rank, or of far greater merit, ever loved or was loved by.

Now I am shamed and afraid because of it, and lie awake and weep and sigh, and hold the dream a great folly, nor believe that it can come true ; yet I cannot drive away from my foolish mind an ambitious, proud, and audacious thought—for I believe that after our voyage the dream will be fulfilled just as it was told to me.

And then you shall hear a singer and songs going and coming. For now—for I am not inspired here—I will pluck up a little more courage to send my messenger who shall bring our greetings to one another ; on my side half the matter is settled, but I have no pledge from her, and I do not think any matter can ever be completed before it is begun.

For I have seen the building of a tower begun with a single stone, and little by little it rises higher until one may furnish it ; wherefore I will maintain my chivalrousness if you advise me thus, and I will send the song on its journey when it is well set to music, if I can find some one who shall carry it there swiftly for me, so that she may rejoice and delight in it.

And if I ever go to an Emperor or to a King, if he wishes to reward me as if I were a traitor, who cannot and knows not how to defend him and maintain him, may he send me away as a hostage to a foreign land ! For I should be thus punished and certain of great harm if the fair lady, white and precious, is harsh to me and remains wroth with me.

And you who know my language must understand and see, if I ever made hidden and closed words, whether I do not now make them very clear.

And I have taken trouble for this, that you may understand the songs I make.

VII

Explanation.—Guiraut de Bornelh had parted from the good King Anfos of Castile, and the King had given him

a very fine grey palfrey and many other gifts, and all the
barons of his court had given him great gifts, and he came
away to Gascony, and he was passing by the country of the
King of Navarre; and the King knew that Guiraut was
thus rich and that he was passing by his country, on the
frontiers of Castile and Aragon and Navarre, and he had
him robbed and all his possessions taken from him, and
he took for his own share the grey palfrey, and the other
booty he left to those who had robbed him. Wherefore
Guiraut made that song, which says: " The sweet song of
a bird."

THE sweet song of a bird that was singing in a hedge drew
          me out of my way the other day, and led me aside, and
          near the enclosure where the little bird was, three
          maidens were lamenting together in a song the excess
          and harm that joy and pleasure have undergone; and
          I went more quickly to hear the song better, and I said
          this to them: " Maidens, of what do you sing, or of
          what do you complain ? "

And the first, who knew most, took up her mantle and said:
          " Of a grief that proceeds from the bad rich men,
          wherefore youth is destroyed; for, as a noble man is a
          guide to nobility, that he may lead it and increase it,
          and bring it forward, so have the worst of wicked men
          set about hurting it, for if you rejoice or make semblance
          of rejoicing, they will treat you so that you may never
          have joy, if you are at all their friend."

" Maiden, the great men are by no means as swift to noble
          enterprises as they were when joy abounded and song
          was welcomed; for I myself—whereat I am grieved—
          find no one who calls to me, or seeks me or asks for me;

but I was robbed this year between the lands of three noble Kings, so that one of the kingdoms wrongs me in it; and that appeared by the grey horse which was kindly given to me and was presented to me in an evil hour."

" My lord, he who robs a paid man and clothes and feeds himself upon his property, loads himself with an evil burden and an evil load, and the place where he is welcomed is much disgraced; if any high lord ever endures or treats well such a wicked thief, full of evil and deceit, he may scarcely be honoured, for those who do not know may very well say to themselves that he himself is inculpated, or that the half falls to his share."

" Friend, men were wont to be gay in the spring season; now they care nothing for an orchard till the fruit fattens it; nor do songs or calls give pleasure. All the world is wretched, and most of all the young men, who do nothing joyful; for I used to see some who for the sake of a glove, if it were sent to them, would start a series of tournaments which lasted the whole year; now they will refuse you their foolish friendship, after honour was taken away from them."

" My lord, the strong castles, where the evil is born, and the walls and ramparts in all directions, have taken away gifts and banquets; for a man is not well equipped unless he makes a mangonel which projects beyond the gallery; so that afterwards a frantic churl will go crying out all night : ' Awake, for I have heard a noise ! ' And then they will rise up, and you, if you do not rise also, will be blamed."

" And how will it profit me if I rebel, my friend, or if I grow angry ? Think you that the worst of men will be moved

by such little blows ?   Or that a hardened youth, if it
pinches him, will grow better for a little blow from the
rod, or that he will become prudent ?   For a real good,
noble man, if he gives you something, saves up for a
year, and then he will fear the trouble, and will think
himself importuned if you ask aught of him."

" If the lord of Bordeaux, my friend, does not bear the burden
of it, and does not take trouble how the world may not
be entirely abased, it would soon be ruined ; for since
joy has failed I see nothing in all the others fitting
to good nobility ; nor will joy or faith or peace ever
go there where the lord reigns in trouble, for those
who surround him will imitate him, and if joy pleases
him they will rejoice on every side."

"Maiden, I shall give up singing any more this year, if it
pleases my Above-all, for I am not well-starred."

" My lord, I know well that the two Bertrans will tell you
you are ill-advised if you give up singing."

" Maiden, he is dishonoured who loves unloved."

VIII

Alba

" Glorious King, Who Heaven and earth did make,
    Almighty God, Lord, for sweet pity's sake,
    Protect my friend, I pray, who is not deeming
    That sunlight soon will o'er the earth be streaming,
        And soon will come the morning.

" Dear comrade, are you sleeping or awake ?
   Sleep now no more, gently your slumbers break,
   For in the east I see the day-star gleaming
   And I am come to rouse you from your dreaming,
      And soon will come the morning.

" Dear comrade, sleep no more, the bird I hear,
   Who seeks day in the woods, in accents clear
   Singing his song, and singing now I hail you,
   Wake, lest your jealous rival should assail you ;
      And soon will come the morning.

" Dear comrade, to the window now draw near,
   That you may see how bright the skies appear,
   And you will know your true friend does not fail you ;
   Scorn not my warning, let my help avail you ;
      And soon will come the morning.

" Dear comrade, since we parted sleep and ease
   I've taken not, nor risen from my knees,
   But prayed to God, Saint Mary's Son, that never
   He would my loving comrade from me sever :
      And soon will come the morning.

" Dear comrade, I have listened to your pleas
   That I should not let slumber on me seize,
   But through the night-time should be wakeful ever
   —And now to rouse you vainly I endeavour,
      And soon will come the morning."

"Dear faithful friend, I am in such delight,
  I would the day might ne'er dispel the night,
  For my beloved in my arms is lying,
  And in this bliss needs must I be defying
    The jealous and the morning."

NOTES

I. "*Now I have joy, remembering the love.*"

Metrical form.—The rimes of the original remain unchanged from stanza to stanza, and line 7, which rimes with the corresponding line of the other stanzas, has a feminine rime. In other respects the metrical form has been preserved in the translation.

This song is supposed to be one of Guiraut's earliest.

II. "*Honour and love and cherishing.*"

Metrical form.—The original keeps the same rimes throughout.

III. "*But why is it, God help me?*"

Metrical form.—The original is written in stanzas of eight lines, each line having seven syllables, except the seventh, which has only five. Rime system, a b b a c c d d.

Stanza 5, l. 2. "My Commander." A pseudonym for the lady.

Stanza 7, l. 3. "The Countess." The lady here alluded to is, very likely, identical with the Countess of Urgel, to whom Raimbaut d'Aurenga addressed some of his songs.

Tornada. "The King." Probably Alfonso II. of Aragon.

IV. *Lament.*

Metrical form.—The original is written in stanzas of eight lines, the second and fifth lines having four syllables each, the other lines eight syllables. Rime system, a a a b b b c c.

If "Ignaure" was indeed Raimbaut d'Aurenga, this poem must have been written in 1173, the year of Raimbaut's death.

Stanza 2, l. 4. "My-Joy." Pseudonym for another friend of Guiraut's.

Stanza 5, l. 5. "Oliver." This celebrated hero of old French epic is often mentioned by the trobadors as an example of bravery.

Stanza 7, l. 4. "good Master Berenguier." Nothing is known of this Master Berenguier. It appears from the context that he had the reputation of being very truthful.

Second tornada. "My Above-all." Guiraut used this pseudonym for his patron, Raimon Bernart de Rovigna.

V. "*I turn to the honour of God.*"

Metrical form.—Stanzas of nine lines, the first six octosyllabic, the seventh tetrasyllabic, and the last two decasyllabic. The fourth syllable of the eighth line rimes with the corresponding syllable in every other stanza. Rime system, a b b a a b b (c) d d.

Stanza 3, l. 6. "his King." I have taken this to mean God. It is possible that the poet may refer merely to one of the leaders of the expedition, but the religious feeling which permeates the whole song makes the other interpretation seem more natural.

Tornada. "Count Richard." As Guiraut speaks of him thus, the poem must have been written before Richard's accession to the English throne on July 6, 1189.

VI. "*I cannot help turning my tongue.*"

Metrical form.—This is the song from which Bertran de Born (or another) took the form of the song, "I love the spring-tide of the year." Guiraut, like his imitator, keeps the same rimes throughout. In other respects the metrical form of this song resembles exactly that of "I love the spring-tide of the year" (p. 92).

Stanza 1, l. 1. "I cannot help," &c. "Where the tooth aches, the tongue goes," was a Provençal proverb.

Stanza 3, l. 1. "my lord." We may suppose from the explanation that his "lord" was the Prince of Antioch, Boemond III.

Tornadas. Here Guiraut alludes to his having formerly written songs in the "obscure manner."

VII. "*The sweet song of a bird.*"

Metrical form.—Stanzas of fifteen hexasyllabic lines. Rime system a, b c b d d a e e f f e e f f.

Guiraut has chosen a somewhat unusual manner of handling a didactic subject, by writing his sirventes in narrative or rather dialogue form.

Stanza 1, l. 4. Doubtless the three maidens have some allegorical significance, but it is not possible to say what this is.

First tornada. "My Above-all." See note on second tornada of the lament for Ignaure.

Second tornada. "the two Bertrans." According to many commentators, the "two Bertrans" are the trobador Guilhem de San Leydier and his lady who, according to the former's biography, called each other by this name. Kolsen thinks that Guiraut refers to Bertran de Baux I. of Aurenga and his son Bertran. If this is the case the song must have been written as early as 1180, as the elder Bertran died in the winter of 1180–81, and the robber King of Navarre cannot have been Sancho the Strong, who only suc-ceeded his father, Sancho the Wise, in 1194.

VIII. *Alba.*

Metrical form.—That of the original has been exactly preserved in the translation.

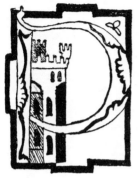

eire Vidal

" Peire Vidal was of Toulouse,
the son of a furrier, and he sang
better than any man in the
world, and he was one of the
most foolish men that ever lived,
for he believed that all things
that pleased him, or that he
wished, were true. And song-
making came more easily to him
than to any man in the world,
and it was he who made the richest melodies and talked
the greatest nonsense about war and love and slandering
of others. And it was true that a knight of Saint Gili cut
his tongue because he gave out that he was his wife's lover.
And Sir Uc del Bauz had him cured and healed. And
when he was cured he went over the seas, and from over
there he brought back a Greek woman who was given him
to wife in Cyprus; and he was given to understand that she
was niece to the Emperor of Constantinople, and that through
her he ought by right to have the Empire, wherefore he
spent all he could gain in making a fleet, for he thought to go
and conquer the Empire. And he had himself called
Emperor and his wife Empress, and he always took about
with him fine steeds and fine arms, and an imperial throne.
And he thought himself the best knight in the world, and
the most loved of ladies; and he fell in love with all the
good ladies he saw, and prayed them all for their love, and
they all said they would do or say what he wanted, wherefore

149

he thought he was the lover of them all, and that every one
would die for him—and they all deceived him

"Peire Vidal, as I have told you, fell in love with all the
good ladies, and thought they all loved him, and he fell in
love with my lady Azalais, who was wife to Sir Barral, Lord
of Marseilles, who bore better will to Peire Vidal than to any
man in the world, because of his song-making and the fine
follies which Peire Vidal said and did.   And they called each
other Rainier.   And Peire Vidal was more intimate in the
court and room of Sir Barral than any man.   And Sir Barral
knew well that Peire Vidal was in love with his wife, and
he held it a jest, as did all those who knew it, and the lady
took it as a jest, as did all the others with whom Peire Vidal
fell in love ; and she spoke him fair and promised him all he
wanted and all he asked for, and he was so wise, that he
believed it all.   And when Peire Vidal grew angry with her,
Sir Barral always made peace, and made her promise all he
asked.   And there came a day when Peire Vidal knew that
Sir Barral had risen and that the lady was all alone in her
room, and he went into the room and came to the bed of
my lady Azalais and found her asleep, and knelt down before
her and kissed her mouth.   And she felt the kiss, and thought
it was Sir Barral, her husband, and smiling she arose; and she
saw it was the fool Peire Vidal, and began to cry out and to
make a great clamour.   And her maidens came from within
when they heard it, and asked, What is this ? and Peire Vidal
ran away.   And the lady sent for Sir Barral, and made great
complaint to him of Peire Vidal, for that he had kissed her,
and weeping she begged him to take vengeance on him.
And Sir Barral, like a noble and a clever man as he was, took
the deed as a joke, laughing and blaming his wife for having
made a clamour about what the fool had done; but he could
not dissuade her from making a great ado about the matter,

and seeking and looking for the wicked Peire Vidal, and she
made great threats against him.

"Peire Vidal for fear entered into a ship and went away to
Genoa, and there he remained, until afterwards he voyaged
across the seas with King Richard, for he went in fear of his
life. There he remained a long time, and there he made
many good songs, recalling the kiss that he had stolen, and
he said in one song that he had had from her 'no reward
save a little knot of ribbon—and yet I had; for one morning
I entered into her house and kissed her like a thief on the
mouth and on the chin.' And in another place he said:
'I should be more honoured than any man born if the stolen
kiss were given to me and fairly acquitted.' And in another
song he said: 'Love beats me well with the rods that I
gather, for once in her royal castle I stole a kiss from her
which I remember full well—alas, so wretched is he who
sees not her he loves.'

"Thus he remained a long time across the seas, for he dared
not return to Provence, and Sir Barral, who bore him such
good will as you have heard, prayed his wife so much that
she pardoned him the kiss and granted it to him as a gift.
And Sir Barral sent for Peire Vidal, and sent him grace and
good will from his wife, and he came with great joy to Marseilles and was very well received by both of them, and
everything was pardoned him, wherefore Peire Vidal made
that song which says: 'Since I have returned to Provence.'

"Peire Vidal was much grieved at the death of the good
Count Raimon of Toulouse, and had great sorrow for it,
and he clad himself in black, and cut off the tails and the ears
of all his horses; and he had his own and all his servants'
heads shaved, but he did not have their beards or their nails
shorn. He went for a long season in the manner of a crazed
man and a sorrowful, and it happened during the time that

he was thus sorrowing that King Anfos of Aragon came to
Provence, and all the good men of his country came with
him, and they found Peire Vidal thus sad and sorrowful, and
arrayed like a man sorrowful and crazed. And the King
and all the barons who were his special friends began to beg
him to give up this grieving and to sing and rejoice, and to
make a song that they might take back to Aragon. The
King and his barons prayed him so much that he said he
would rejoice and give up his mourning, and would make a
song, and do all they wished.

"And he loved the Loba of Puegnautier, and my lady
Estofania, who was of Cerdagne, and now again he fell in
love with my lady Raimbauda de Biol, wife of Sir Guilhem
Rostanh de Biol (Biol is in Provence). Now the Loba [1]
was of the country hard by Carcassonne, and Peire Vidal
had himself called Wolf for her sake, and he bore the
arms of a wolf, and in the mountain of Cabaret he had himself hunted by the shepherds with mastiffs and greyhounds,
as one hunts a wolf. And he donned a wolfskin to give the
shepherds and the dogs to understand that he was a wolf.
And the shepherds with their dogs chased him, and entreated
him so cruelly that he was carried away for dead to the house
of the Loba of Puegnautier. When she knew that this was
Peire Vidal she began to rejoice greatly over the folly that
Peire Vidal had done, and to laugh much, and her husband
also. And they received him with great amusement, and
the husband had him put in a place apart, as well as he could,
and sent for the doctor, and had him tended until he was
healed.

"And as I began to tell you about Peire Vidal, that he had
promised the King and his barons to make a song ; when he

---

[1] *Loba* means "she-wolf" in Provençal.

was cured the King had arms made for himself and for Peire Vidal, and he was very well pleased, and he made that song which says : ' I had given up singing for sorrow and grief.' "

Such is the rambling account of Peire Vidal's life given in the MSS. Some of it may have been invented from allusions in his songs, but it is possible that every word is true, for Peire Vidal seems to have been a possessor of that genius which is akin to madness. Many of his songs are of such excellence as to entitle him to rank with the very best of Provençal poets, others display a conceit so ludicrous as to incline one to believe all the absurd stories that are told of the author. Peire Vidal was a riddle to his contemporaries, who could not understand how a man who wrote such good poetry, and said so many sensible things in verse, could behave like a crazy fool. Perhaps his head was turned by success and flattery, for he seems to have been immensely popular at the numerous courts he visited—greatly, no doubt, on account of his " fine follies." He went to many other places besides those mentioned in the biography, and visited more different countries than any of his literary contemporaries. Diez, Bartsch, and Schopf have all tried to trace his wanderings by means of his songs and the historical events alluded to in them.

Born about the middle of the twelfth century, he spent his earliest years in the south of France. It is not known when he first began to make songs, but the earliest we possess are addressed to Azalais of Marseilles ; so the court of Barral de Baux, the Viscount of Marseilles, must have been one of the first he visited. He seems to have gone to Spain early in his career, probably at the invitation of King Alfonso II. of Aragon, but to have returned soon to Southern France, to have visited Toulouse, Biolh (Beuil), and Carcassonne, and

then to have gone back to Marseilles. He sang the praises
of many ladies, but his love for the Viscountess of Marseilles
was greater and more lasting than any of his other passions.
Several trobadors sang of her, and she seems to have been
equally indifferent to them all. Indeed her husband, Barral,
gave them more encouragement than she did. He was
famous for his generous patronage of the trobadors, and
Peire Vidal was clearly a favourite of his. In 1181 he wrote
a sirventes dealing with the war between Alfonso of Aragon
and Raimon of Toulouse, his sympathies being with the King.
Some time after this there occurred the episode of the stolen
kiss, and the trobador's banishment from Marseilles. According to Schopf, it was at this time that he went to Cyprus
and married his Greek wife. Probably he returned to France
about 1188, and went to Marseilles in the following year,
having been forgiven by Azalais. It is not certain how
long he remained there, but he must have left before 1192,
as Barral died in that year, and Peire makes no mention of
his death, which he would certainly have done had he been
in Marseilles at the time. He was in the Carcassonne district
in 1193, singing the praises of Loba, and this year, probably,
was the date of the "wolf-hunt." In 1194 Count Raimon V.
of Toulouse died, and Peire, according to the biography,
mourned him in characteristically eccentric fashion until
King Alfonso of Aragon persuaded him to take up singing
again. In the song which he wrote in compliance with the
King's request, he mentions the wolf-hunt.

About this time Peire discovered, in common with the
rest of the world, that he had a favoured rival for the affec-
tions of Loba in the person of Count Roger Raimon of Foix.
Thereupon he renounced her, and then went to the Court
of the Marquis Boniface of Montferrat.

In 1196 Alfonso of Aragon died, and soon afterwards Peire

visited the court of King Emmerich of Hungary, son-in-law
of Alfonso.   Returned from there, he seems to have gone to
Spain again, but on hearing of Boniface of Montferrat's
projected Crusade (1202), he wrote a song encouraging it.
Opinions are divided as to whether he accompanied the
Marquis to the East, but in 1204 he was at Malta.   He seems
to have spent the last years of his life with Blacatz, a noted
patron of the trobadors.   The year of his death is not
known ; it was probably about 1208 or 1210.

Peire Vidal was one of the best of Provençal poets.   Like
Bernart of Ventadorn, he was able to combine rich and
elaborate metrical forms with perfect clearness and simplicity of expression.   The "obscure manner" which
Arnaut Daniel made so fashionable at this time found little
favour with him, he preferred to make his songs melodious to
the ear and simple to the understanding.   He was fond of
refrain words and lines, as we shall notice in the songs translated below.   His great fault is a habit of treating more
than one subject in a single poem.   The *canso-sirventes*, a
song dealing partly with love and partly with politics or
social matters, was a recognised *genre* of Provençal lyric poetry,
but it was an inartistic form, and it is to be regretted that
Peire Vidal used it so often.   If we may judge by his wandering life, he had a restless disposition, and perhaps this rest-
lessness finds expression in some of his poems, in which he is
continually hovering between one subject and another.

I

> I LOVE lark and nightingale
> More than other birds that sing,
> Who, for joy they have in spring,
> First of all their voices raise.

And I have the self-same ways,
For, when others' songs we miss,
I alone do sing of bliss
All for love of my Vierna.

And, that pity may prevail
When my songs to her I bring,
I'll do well in everything,
For in truth I'm hers always
From henceforward, for she says
That her slave she won't dismiss,
So that evermore, I wis,
I shall stay near my Vierna.

Ah, the hurt I now bewail
Wounds me more than stone from sling,
Sharper than a knife's the sting;
And indeed he earns dispraise
Who unasked his love displays,
And a lady does amiss
Who loves riches—and from this
May God save my fair Vierna.

II

If I were in a court of law, I'd bring
Complaint against my lady, though she be
So good and fair, for she ill-treats me so,
She keeps not pledge or covenant she's made.
Why does she promise what she will not cede?
Fears she not wrong, knows she not it is shame?

'Twere better had she been at first unkind
Than that I now should feel her rancour's sting,
But as a charmer has she treated me,
For with fair looks she's plunged me deep in woe
From which there's no escape without her aid
—'Tis pity she's so good and fair indeed !

In other things she's courteous and polite,
But wrong it is my harm to have designed,
For she gives me more ceaseless suffering
Than toothache when it hurts most grievously.
My love for her strikes my heart many a blow
For her sake and Provence's, whence I've strayed.

And, since I see not Rainier of Marseilles,
Although I live, no life's my grievous plight ;
The sick man who in long relapse has pined
Will die if his disease be lingering ;
So I, if of desire I can't be free,
Which takes my breath away, shall die I know.

Full late, meseems, my love I shall have won,
No lady, sure, more cruelly assails
Her slave ; though her I serve with all my might,
The more I do, the harsher her I find.
A greater fool am I, thus worshipping,
Than foolish shepherd piping to the lea.

He whom love overpowers endures defeat ;
I, when I saw my lady, was undone ;
None can compare with her, for she prevails
O'er all in merit rare and beauty bright.
My whole life's love is hers ; if she's not kind,
Indeed 'twill be a wrong and unjust thing.

Now go your way, song, to the noble Queen
In Aragon, no true Queen can I meet
Save her in all the world, though many a one
I've sought, but every one in something fails,
But she is true and noble, the delight
Of every one, and pleasing in God's mind.

And since the King above all Kings is great,
True, such a King well merits such a Queen.

Fair Castiatz, your merit is worth more
Than others', for more good deeds make it great.

God save my lady and my Gazanhat,
For none so well as he makes gifts or war.

III

BARONS, I challenge false disloyal slanderers to harm me, for
I have chosen a lady in whom there is true beauty, and
I love her with a true heart and without deceit, and I
am all hers, whenever she may be mine, for her beauty
and her merit appear before all, for she was never reluctant to love, wherefore I am rich if she deign to say
" yes " to me.

Nothing has pleased me so well as the joyous true lady, in
whom is every good quality and all good without any
evil. Since all things are in her that are befitting to
love, I am lucky if only I may be there, and if mercy,
which makes all good things to increase, avail me aught
with her, I may well say without any denial that I never
could effect so much with love.

Singing and pleasure I see at an end, courts and gifts and fair dwellings, and I do not see wooing approved of, unless the lady or the lover be false. For he gains most who deceives oftenest—I will say no more, but let things go as they will. But it grieves me much that the first false man who ever began to act thus was not at once annihilated, and it would have been justice, for he started a bad example.

My heart is rejoiced because Sir Barral will have me again ; good luck to her who brought me up, and to God, for I am such an one that a thousand greetings come to me every day from Catalonia and from Lombardy, for every day my value mounts and increases, wherefore the King nearly dies of envy, for I have my fun and my pleasure with ladies.

It is indeed proved and known how noble and distinguished I am, and since God has enriched me it is not fitting that I should be venal. I know of a hundred ladies each of whom would fain have me with her, could she but get me—but I am one who never boasted or made pretensions, nor do I like to talk too much about myself, but I kiss ladies and overthrow knights.

Many a good tourney have I taken part in with the deadly blows I strike, for I can go nowhere without men crying out, " This is Sir Peire Vidal, he who maintains wooing and love, and acts as a noble man for love of his lady, and loves battles and tourneys more than a monk loves peace, and grows sick of resting and remaining too long in one place."

No more than a fish can live without water can wooing be without slanderers.

IV

When the wind is gently blowing
From Provence, I drink the breezes;
All that comes from there so pleases
Me, when I hear men bestowing
Praise on it, I fain would hear
Hundred times as much, for sheer
Joy it is to hear its praises.

Fairer land is no man knowing
Than that land across the seas is
—Where she dwells who my heart's ease is—
'Twixt Vence and the Rhône swift-flowing;
Wherefore 'mid those people dear
I have left my glad heart, near
Her who grief to gladness raises.

Soon can she be overthrowing
Grief, if on one's heart it seizes;
E'en the thought of her appeases
Woe, and he whose praise is glowing
Never to speak false need fear;
Sure it is she has no peer,
None so fair in mirror gazes.

And if wit and art I'm showing,
Then my gratitude for these is
Due to her, for all one sees is
To her inspiration owing;
All that I do well, 'tis clear,
Comes from her alone, the mere
Thought of whom my heart amazes.

V

No man can save himself from love when he has put himself
under Love's command; whether it please him or
not he must obey his wishes. And you must know
that a man in love cannot follow any other wish, but
he hastens wherever Love wills, and heeds neither sense
nor folly in it.

Then I knew little of defending myself, for I never took
heed until I was caught like a foolish bird when it hears
the decoy and goes quickly to its death. And I rushed
headlong into such a snare, wherefore I now think
myself deceived, for I am in the power of a lord who
will not do me good or honour.

A man should fly from nothing more than from a bad master
if he can, but I cannot fly from mine at all, for Love
went beyond the seas to strike me on the left side such
a blow that I have returned here because of it, wherefore
I shall die of grief and sorrow if true joy does not
help me.

And my lady, if she so willed, could cure me of sorrow
with joy, and by my faith if it so pleased her my death
ought not to delight her. For I am utterly in her
power, and you must know I do not say this because I
fear death, but because she loses her lover.

Indeed my lady should recognise how I have returned to
her mercy, for, by right, good faith should avail where
power of serving fails. For in great courts pity excuses
the most guilty, wherefore humility with nobility gives
a sweet savour to all other joys.

I should be able to cure myself of any other ill, but I myself
cut the bridle of this one when my fair lady promised
me that concerning which she had it in her heart to
lie to me. And ill-rewarded service—it is a great sin
to accept it, for many a good servant is poor because
of bad rewarders.

Lady, I can endure no more; might God and kindness
help me, that I might gain some good from you, for
I have not the power to desire anything else. Your
great beauty oppresses me so that it has invaded my
eyes and passed them so that I have the splendour
of it in my head, and it takes wits and strength from me.

Lord Count of Poitou, it pleases me well that you have
mounted the highest step, for I see you nobly regaining
the honour your ancestors lost.

Although my Castiatz is wicked, I have grief and pity for
him, for he is old and is dishonoured, and takes Lady
Vierna and her love from me.

VI

Full well I like the season bright and good,
I like the lovely summer-time to see,
I like the birds when they sing piously,
I like the flowers growing in the wood.
I like all things on which the good set store,
I like sweet converse many score times more,
Wherefore soon, as I like, I shall rejoice
Where, as I like, I've set my heart and voice.

Love keeps me ever happy and full glad,
Love keeps me in a fever-heat of joy,
Love keeps me brave and free from all annoy,
For love's sake I am pensive oft and sad.
For love's sake I'm so deep in love that nought
But love has place in every wish and thought,
For love's sake I love courtesy and youth,
For all I do is done for love in truth.

'Tis well with me, love, when I think on you,
And well, since I am under your command,
'Tis well to hear your praise on every hand,
And well, when your fair countenance I view.
'Tis well when I look on your loveliness,
And well, because your power I confess,
'Tis well with me that all my thoughts you own,
Well that I love you only and alone.

God save you, lady, fair and virtuous,
But save not seekers after strife and wrong,
And God save me, since to you I belong,
But save not jealous men or slanderous.
God save the good, the clever and the brave,
But cursed dullards may He never save,
God save all lovers when their love is true,
But save not those who falsehood say or do.

Lady, to see you I'm so suffering,
Lady, no thought else in my heart can be,
Lady, for you can make a slave of me,
Lady, or richer than Anfos the King.

Good lady, now your power is complete,
Lady, my heart and will are at your feet;
Lady, regard my pleading if you will,
Lady, that pity your true heart may fill.

True, pure joy, made of love and of delight,
With joy of you all good things live again,
No joy so pleasing doth the world contain,
For your joy makes the world's life gay and bright.
From you joy springs and grows on without end,
Whence I have joy and Castiatz my friend.
Great joy I have whene'er I hear him tell
The joy of you who do all things so well.

VII

GOOD luck to me, who can conceal
My grief with joyous mien,
Good luck to me, because I feel
No anger, 'spite my teen.
Good luck to me, who love and will not leave her,
Good luck to me, who never will deceive her,
Good luck to me, because I love the Queen
Of beauty, and the noblest ever seen,
And ill luck to the jealous.

Good luck to me, who can delight
One who's so fair to see,
Good luck to me, who can requite
Those who do good to me.
Good luck to me, who hide my true love ever,
Good luck to me since base men please me never,
Good luck to me above all men that be,
For never lover slept so happily,
And ill-luck to the jealous.

Good luck to me and to my sighs,
For they are sweet, though deep,
Good luck to me, who can despise
Grief, and hold comfort cheap.
Good luck to me and to her mother's daughter,
Good luck to me since love and praise I've brought her,
Good luck to me—and may the slanderers reap
Sorrow, for I will sing whoe'er may weep,
And ill-luck to the jealous.

Good luck to me if e'er I dare
Disclose my passion's flame,
Good luck to me if she can bear
To hear me without blame,
Good luck to me, since I know where she's living,
Good luck to me if my song's pleasure giving,
Good luck to me who have her servant's name,
For nevermore my bondage I'll disclaim,
And ill luck to the jealous.

Good luck to me whose heart always
Is at my lady's feet,
Good luck to me who, when I praise
Her, can say no deceit.
Good luck to me and good luck to another,
Good luck to me and to my lady mother,
Good luck to me and better to my sweet,
And God save good King Peire as is meet,
And ill luck to the jealous.

Perchat, to Audiart go swift and fleet,
I know but one whom I love more to greet,
And ill luck to the jealous.

NOTES

I. "*I love lark and nightingale.*"

Metrical form.—That of the original has been exactly preserved
in the translation. Note the refrain "my Vierna" at the end of
each stanza.

This is one of Peire Vidal's earliest songs; it was written during
his first stay at Marseilles.

He uses the name "Vierna" to designate the Viscountess.

II. "*If I were in a court of law.*"

Metrical form.—That of the original has been exactly preserved
in the translation, except that masculine rimes have been substi-
tuted for feminine. In this poem, Peire imitates Arnaut Daniel's
device of leaving his lines unrimed till the following stanzas, and
improves on it, altering the position of the rimes from stanza to
stanza by introducing a fresh rime-word in the first line of each
stanza.

According to Schopf this song was written soon after Peire's
first visit to Spain and before he returned to Marseilles. Bartsch
assigns it to a later period—after his return from Cyprus—and
thinks the cruel lady is Loba and not Azalais.

Stanza 4, l. 1. "Rainier of Marseilles." Barral de Baux.
The Provençal biography (see p. 150) tells us that Barral and
Peire called each other by this name. It was a common practice
among friends to have a mutual assumed name.

Stanza 7, l. 1. "the noble Queen." The wife of his patron
Alfonso II. of Aragon, Sancha, daughter of Alfonso VII. of Castile.

Second Tornada. "Castiatz." He often alludes to this patron,
whose identity is not known. Neither is it known who the
"Gazanhat" of the third tornada may be.

III. "*Barons, I challenge.*"

Metrical form.—Stanzas of nine lines, the first four lines
octosyllabic, the rest decasyllabic. The fifth and sixth lines

have feminine endings, the rest masculine. Rime system, a b a b c˘c˘d d e.

This song gives an amusing illustration of Peire Vidal's overpowering vanity. He extols himself in all seriousness as the bravest of knights and the most gallant of wooers. Probably it was written when he was actually on his way to Marseilles for the second time.

IV. *"When the wind is gently blowing,"*

Metrical form.—That of the original has been exactly reproduced. This song was written during Peire's banishment from Marseilles. Stanza 2, ll. 3 and 4. "that land. . . . 'twixt Vence and the Rhône." The Viscounty of Marseilles, situated between Vence (Alpes Maritimes) and the Rhône.

V. *"No man can save himself from love."*

Metrical form.—Stanzas of eight octosyllabic lines. Rime system, a b b a c c d d.

First Tornada. "Lord Count of Poitou." Richard, who had just succeeded to the throne of England. The allusion to Richard's accession enables us to assign a fairly definite date to the poem. Most probably it was written in the late summer of 1189 (Henry II. died on July 6th). It appears from the contents of the poem that it was written after Peire's return from the East to France, but before Azalais had pardoned him for the theft of the kiss.

Second Tornada. The meaning of these lines is not very clear. It would appear from them that the poet's friend "Castiatz" had prevented a reconciliation between Peire and his lady.

VI. *"Full well I like the season bright."*

Metrical form.—The rimes in the original remain unchanged.

In this song we have a variant of the use of a refrain word, a particular word or expression occurring in every line of a stanza.

Most likely it was written shortly before Peire's return to Marseilles.

Stanza 5, l. 4. "Anfos the King." Most likely Alfonso II. of Aragon.

VII. " *Good luck to me.*"

Metrical form.—In the original the rimes remain unchanged.

Bartsch assigns this song to the last years of Peire's life. Schopf thinks he is not the author, as it is only preserved in one MS., and the names Audiart and Perchat do not occur elsewhere in his works. But both form and style are suggestive of Peire. We have the refrain, and the self-complacency of the author is characteristic of Peire.

It is not known who the lady addressed may have been.

Stanza 5, l. 8. "King Peire." Pedro II. of Aragon, son and successor of Alfonso II.

uilhem de Cabestanh

GUILHEM DE CABESTANH is better known by
the romantic story told of his love and
death than by his poems.

Several different versions of this story
are given in the MSS., the simplest being
as follows :—

"Guilhem de Cabestanh was a knight of the country of
Rossilhon, which borders on Catalonia and on Narbonnais.
He was a very handsome man, and well skilled in arms and in
courtesy and in serving. And in his country there was a
lady whose name was my lady Soremonda, wife of Sir Raimon
de Castel-Rossilhon, who was a very noble and powerful man,
and wicked and cruel, and fierce and proud. And Sir
Guilhem de Cabestanh loved the lady and sang of her, and
made his songs of her; and the lady, who was young and gay,
and noble and beautiful, bore better will to him than to
any one in the world. And it was told to Sir Raimon de
Castel-Rossilhon, and he, like an angry and a jealous man,
inquired about the matter and found that it was true, and
he had his wife guarded. And on a day Raimon de Castel-
Rossilhon met Guilhem de Cabestanh passing by and slew
him, and had his heart taken from his body, and had his
head cut off, and he had the head and the heart carried to his
house. He caused the heart to be roasted and seasoned, and
had it given to his wife to eat. And when the lady had eaten
it Raimon de Castel-Rossilhon said to her, 'Do you know
what you have eaten?' And she said to him, 'No, save that
it was very good meat, and well flavoured.' And he told

her that it was of a truth the heart of Sir Guilhem de
Cabestanh that she had eaten ; and so that she might well
believe it, he had the head brought before her.   And when
the lady saw and heard this, she forthwith lost sight and
hearing, and when she came to, she said, ' My lord, you have
indeed given me such good food that nevermore will I eat
of any other.'   And when he heard this, he rushed at her
with his sword, and tried to strike her on the head, and she
ran to a balcony and let herself fall down ; and thus she
died.   The news spread throughout Rossilhon and the
whole of Catalonia that Sir Guilhem de Cabestanh and the
lady were thus cruelly killed, and that Sir Raimon de Castel-
Rossilhon had given the heart of Sir Guilhem to the lady to
eat.   There was very great grief and sorrow thereat throughout all the country, and the complaint came before the King
of Aragon, who was overlord of Sir Raimon de Castel-
Rossilhon and of Sir Guilhem de Cabestanh ; and he came
to Perpignan in Rossilhon and made Raimon de Castel-
Rossilhon come before him.   And when he had come, he caused
him to be seized, and took his castles from him and had them
destroyed, and took from him everything he had, and led
him away to prison.   He caused Guilhem de Cabestanh
and the lady to be taken and carried to Perpignan and buried
in a tomb before the door of the church, and he caused the
manner of their death to be inscribed on the tomb ; and he
commanded throughout the county of Rossilhon that all
the knights and the ladies should come to make a pilgrimage
to them every year.   And Sir Raimon de Castel-Rossilhon
died miserably in the prison of the King of Aragon."

In two MSS. the story is greatly expanded by the introduction of an episode telling how Guilhem and the lady's
sister succeeded for a time in allaying the husband's suspicions,
and of various conversations between the characters.   In

these versions the lady is called Margarida. Many versions name a particular song, and the exact lines of it, as having excited Raimon's jealousy.

These many different accounts of the same incident suffice alone to cast some doubt on the truth of the story, and there are several other reasons for believing it to be entirely without foundation. The story of the lover's heart being set before the lady by the jealous husband is found in so many forms that it may be dismissed at once as fabulous. Historical documents furnish fairly conclusive proof that Raimon de Castel-Rossilhon never murdered Guilhem de Cabestanh at all. We have the marriage-contract (1197) of Raimon and Soremonda, and also that (1210) of Soremonda, "widow of Raimon de Castel-Rossilhon" and Ademar de Masset. Soremonda was still living in 1221. Guilhem de Cabestanh is mentioned as having taken part in the battle of Las Navas in 1212—Raimon therefore died before either of the others. The King of Aragon, who is said to have avenged the deaths of Guilhem and his lady, is called Anfos in several versions of the biography. The only King Alfonso of Aragon to whom the county of Rossilhon (Roussillon) belonged was Alfonso II., the noted patron of the trobadors, and he died in 1196, a year before the marriage of Raimon and Soremonda.

It seems as if the whole story told of the trobador were derived from some older Provençal novel now lost, itself derived perhaps from the old French *lai* of *Guiron*. This *lai* is also lost, but it is mentioned in Thomas' romance of *Tristran*, from which we learn that it told of a harper, Guiron, who loved a certain Countess and was murdered by her husband, who caused her to eat the heart of Guiron. The story told of the Chastelain de Coucy may be derived from this same *lai*. Gaston Paris thought that Boccaccio's version of the story of Guilhem de Cabestanh (*Decamerone*, IV. 9) was derived not, as is usually supposed, from the "biography" quoted above, but from the same source as that biography, namely some lost Provençal novel. It has never been explained how and when the legend came to be applied to the trobador. There seems no reason for doubting the statement that Guilhem addressed his songs to the wife of Raimon de Castel-Rossilhon, but as far as we can judge from the documents mentioned above there is no other true feature in this most tragic of all trobador biographies.

Only eight of Guilhem's poems have come down to us. These have so much charm that it is to be regretted that more of his work has not survived. In their simplicity and sincerity his songs recall those of Bernart of Ventadorn, although they lack the note of passionate emotion that characterises the work of that great poet. None of his music has survived.

I

LADY, that day when first I saw your face,
When of your grace you first to me were shown,
All other thoughts to thoughts of you gave place,
All my desire centred on you alone.
For, lady, love within my heart you planted
With your sweet smile and with your welcome kind,
So that all else was banished from my mind.

Your radiant beauty and your wondrous grace,
Your greeting sweet, your voice's gentle tone
My heart did in a net of love enlace,
And ne'er since, lady, has it been mine own;
But to advance your praise, who it enchanted,
Is the sweet task I have to it assigned,
For ne'er a love more worthy shall I find.

Lady, I love so truly that all trace
Of other love far from my heart has flown,
Yet I have courted others for a space,
Thinking my grief thus to have overthrown.
But thoughts of you, in whom all joy's implanted,
Soon to all other love do make me blind,
And to oblivion is the world consigned.

Do not that promise from your thoughts efface
Which when we parted you to me made known ;
Such joy it gave me that now grows apace
The seed of hope that in my heart was sown.
Some day I shall achieve what I have wanted
So long, and then will grief be left behind,
When you again to mercy are inclined.

Gladly I suffer cruelty, in case
I may thereby gain that which will atone
For all—a kindly look, or an embrace,
For sake of which all harshness I condone.
A faithful lover ever takes for granted
That joy will come to him who's not repined,
Though love is not to joy alone confined.

Ah, lady dear, whose praise so long I've chanted,
When will you call me friend, and closer bind
The lover who so long for you has pined ?

II

I NEVER thought that I should leave amusement for love,
    or singing for joy, or that I should weep for very delight ;

Love holds me fast in her power who begins many sweet delights in my heart, and I think God created me for her service and for her needs.

For I often complain of things about which I make a song of praise, and I thank her for that which I ought to complain of ; I do it not to deceive, but he whom Love graces ought to endure many things, for it often happens that evil is necessary, that good may overcome it.

A lover who is always changing his bearing ought not to complain of suffering or to speak of his grief, or to make his loss known or to praise the goodness that is shown him. Many speak at once who do not even know from whence joy or displeasure come.

You absorb my thoughts so much that often when I am saying my prayers I think I am before you, for I have your fresh colour and your graceful body so much in my remembrance that I remember nothing else ; from this sweet thought nobility and good-will come to me.

III

THE sweet thought that love often gives me, lady, makes me say many pleasing songs of you. Thoughtful I gaze upon your fair body, which I love and desire more than I appear to, and though I seem faithless for your sake I do not abjure you, for I soon entreat you with true good-will. Lady whom beauty makes bright, many times I forget myself, for I praise you and ask mercy.

May love, which you forbid me, always be wroth with me if I ever turn my heart towards another affection. You have taken laughter from me and given me care. No man feels greater torment than I, for in appearance I blame and disbelieve, and cease to love you whom I long for more than any woman in the world ; all that I do through fear you ought to take in good faith, even when I do not see you.

I keep in remembrance your face and your sweet smile, your value and your fair, slim, white body ; if I were so true in my belief in God, I should enter into Paradise in my lifetime without fail, for thus have I surrendered myself to you with my whole heart, so that no other woman brings joy to me, for there is none whose whole love I would care for in exchange for your salutation.

Always my desire pleases me, for your bearing delights me so much, you whom I worship. Indeed it seems to me that your love conquers me, for before I ever saw you it was my intention to love and to serve you. For thus have I remained here without any help for your sake, and I have lost many gifts thereby—whoever wants them may have them ! I like better to wait for you, from whom joy came to me, without any settled agreement.

Before grief may be enkindled in my heart, may mercy descend on you, lady, and love ; may joy give you to me and send sighs and tears from me ; let neither rank nor wealth forbid you to me, for all good is forgotten by me if mercy on me is of no avail with you. Ah, fair, sweet lady, it were very great kindness if you had loved me the very first time I had asked you, or not at all, for now I know not how it is.

I find no contradiction to your value, may such pity seize you for this as shall do you honour. May God never

hear me among His suppliants if I would take the
revenue of the four greatest Kings if so mercy and good
faith did not avail me with you ; for I cannot by any
means depart from you in whom my love is placed,
and if it were captured while kissing, and it pleased you,
I would never wish to be delivered.

Nothing that pleased you, noble and courteous lady, would
be so impossible to me that I would not do it before I
remembered anything else.

Sir Raimon, the beauty and the goodness which are in my
lady have bound and imprisoned me here.

IV

THE sweet voice in the wood rejoices me when it resounds
on the budding branch, and the nightingale warbles
his song beside his mate as he is wont, and I hear the
bird's song echoing ; then I remember the sweet land
and country, and the charm of my joyful lady, where
fore I ought indeed to rejoice, if I could.

Indeed I ought to have great joy in my heart, since all great
worth is to be found in my lady and she envies no other
for her beauty ; of such fair estate did God make her
that if she were among her enemies they could not say
that such a fair one ever lived ; wisdom is in her, beauty
and courtesy, no man sees her who cannot say a hundred
times better things of her.

I will go to make my home in another country, so that I
may never stay in this one, and the slanderers who have
killed me with envy will have great joy when they see

me wandering. And I will go away as a poor pilgrim, and my desires will soon have killed me, and though I have never served Love well, yet I will serve you all the days of my life.

Go, my sigh, as a true messenger, straight to my lady to whom all true worth devotes itself, and tell her that I desire no other, and that I do not make obeisance to any other power; when I think of her lovely eyes and her face, I nearly die if I must part from her. I neither should or could ever part from her, but my heart is with her night and day.

V

Love keeps me pondering how I may best
Compose for my belov'd a joyous song,
For her to whom my heart and soul belong,
Whom Love made me to choose from all the rest,
And whom he hath ordained I must adore
And serve and honour faithfully and purely;
And so I do, my love for her full surely
From day to day grows better and grows more.

Full well has Love cured me of the despair
Which long he made me suffer, and the woe;
Unjust it was of him to treat me so,
For almost I was forced to turn elsewhere.
If he is wise, now let him bear in mind
That in a little while luck often changes;
He who ill-treats his subjects oft estranges
Others who'd serve him well if he were kind.

For you must know, my lords, I have heard tell
How once a powerful Emperor of yore
Oppressed his barons grievously, wherefore
His pride was humbled and his power fell.
And so I pray my noble beauteous one
Not to ill-treat her lover too extremely,
For gentleness in everything is seemly,
And one repents too late when harm is done.

Dear lady, best of all the best that be,
In whom all charm and all delight do meet,
Love for your sake holds me in prison sweet ;
I tell you this that it may profit me.
God grant me life until the day is past
When I shall lie within your arms' embraces,
For unto me than this no greater grace is
In all the world, and while the world shall last.

And lady, since of treasure you've great store
—For the world holds none nobler or more fair—
Let not, I pray, my true love and my care
Be vain ; the richer a man is, the more
Should he reward good service which men do,
For it is just and right, I tell you truly,
Evil should be repaid by evil duly
And good by good—nought else I ask of you.

My tears and sighs have been a thousand quite,
Alas, so fear I nought to gain of worth
When I reflect upon your noble birth
And how you are of all the flower and light,

And how I know you precious, sweet and fair,
And how you are true, pure, in faith unbroken,
And how by all men it is sworn and spoken
That never woman like you breathed the air.

Take pity of your goodness on my plight,
Heed not your greatness, lady, but have care
For the true love that in my heart you've woken,
And for my faith that never will be broken,
Since all my love for you alone I bear.

NOTES

I. "*Lady, that day when first I saw your face.*"

Metrical form.—That of the original has been exactly preserved in the translation.

II. "*I never thought.*"

Metrical form.—The original is written in stanzas of nine hexasyllabic lines, the sixth and ninth feminine, the rest masculine. Rime system, a b a b a c˘d d c˘.

III. "*The sweet thought.*"

Metrical form.—Stanzas of fifteen lines. The first eight lines have alternate feminine tetrasyllabic and masculine hexasyllabic lines, lines 9–11 have masculine hexasyllabic, 12 and 13 feminine hexasyllabic, and 14 and 15 masculine hexasyllabic lines. Rime system, a˘b a˘b a˘b a˘b c c c d˘d˘c c. The same rime endings remain for two stanzas, then rime d˘is used as rime a˘ for the third and fourth stanzas, the other lines having fresh rimes arranged as in the preceding stanzas. A similar change takes place at the fifth stanza.

This song, the most celebrated of Guilhem's poems, was, according to some versions of the biography, the means of betraying the love of Guilhem and his lady to Raimon de Castel-Rossilhon. Some MSS. even point out the special passage that confirmed Raimon's suspicions. This passage is at the end of stanza 2—"all that I do through fear you ought to take in good faith, even when I do not see you."

The fact that the second tornada of this very song is addressed to Raimon is further evidence of the baselessness of the whole story.

IV. "*The sweet voice in the wood.*"

Metrical form.—Stanzas of eight decasyllabic lines; the fifth and sixth masculine, the rest feminine. Rime system, a˘b˘b˘a˘c c d˘d˘.

V. "*Love keeps me pondering how I may best.*"

Metrical form.—The original keeps the same rimes throughout.

Two Anonymous Albas

I

Within an orchard, 'neath the mayflowers white,
Two lovers dreamed away the livelong night,
Until the watcher cries the East grows light.
Ah God, ah God, the dawn, how soon it comes!

"Would God the night might never yield to morn,
And that my love might leave me not forlorn,
And that the watcher ne'er might see the dawn.
Ah God, ah God, the dawn, how soon it comes!

"Beloved, when I kiss thee, kiss thou me,
While in the fields the birds make melody;
Let us do this in spite of jealousy.
Ah God, ah God, the dawn, how soon it comes!

"Beloved, let us dream together here,
Within the garden, where the birds sing clear,
Until the watcher warns us day is near.
Ah God, ah God, the dawn, how soon it comes!

"Sweet is the breeze that wafts to me the kiss
Of my fair joyous love, and it is bliss
To drink his sweet breath with my lips like this.
Ah God, ah God, the dawn, how soon it comes!"

Gentle the lady is, and courteous too,
And many men her beauty love to view;
Her heart is given to faithful love and true.
Ah God, ah God, the dawn, how soon it comes!

II

WHEN the nightingale is crying
To his mate, and she replying,
My true love and I are lying
        'Mid the flowers,
Till the watcher from the towers
Calls out: " Lovers, now arise!
I see daylight in the skies."

NOTES

I. and II.

Metrical form.—That of both originals has been exactly preserved in the translation.

We have already met with an example of this *genre* among the works of Guiraut de Bornelh.

The originals of the above translations are preserved in only one MS., and it is quite impossible to tell who may have written them. The longer alba is perhaps the most beautiful specimen of Provençal verse that has come down to us.   The refrain of Swinburne's poem " In the Orchard " (Poems and Ballads, First Series), " Ah God, ah God, that day should be so soon," is borrowed from it.

INDEX

THE END